D1738510

Back To School At My Age?

A Guide for Both the Returning Student and the College Administrator

Del Witherspoon
Auburn University at Montgomery

Eugenie Nickell
Northwest Albama Mental Health Center

Introduction by
Guinevera A. Nance, Ph.D.

Includes Personal Stories by
Angie Eason & Gail Hood

UNIVERSITY
PRESS OF
AMERICA

Lanham • New York • London

Copyright © 1991 by
University Press of America®, Inc.
4720 Boston Way
Lanham, Maryland 20706

3 Henrietta Street
London WC2E 8LU England

Library of Congress Cataloging-in-Publication Data

Back to school at my age? : a guide for both the returning student
and the college administrator / edited by Del Witherspoon and
Eugenie Nickell ; introduction by Guinevera A. Nance.
p.   cm.
Includes bibliographical references
1. Adult education—United States—Psychological aspects.
2. College student orientation—United States.
3. Personnel service in adult education—United States.
4. Universities and colleges—United States—Administration.
5. Study, Method of.
I. Witherspoon, Del, 1940- .   II. Nickell, Eugenie.
LC5225.P78B33   1991   374'.973—dc20   91-24469 CIP

ISBN 0-8191-8412-8 (cloth, alk. paper)
ISBN 0-8191-8413-6 (pbk., alk. paper)

DEDICATION

This book is dedicated to individuals who are considering returning to school or have already begun their educational pursuits. While we share your apprehensions, we encourage and applaud your efforts toward personal achievements -- achievements well worth the time, expense, and sacrifice.

ACKNOWLEDGEMENTS

We extend our appreciation to each of the authors of the chapters for their efforts and patience as we pursued deadlines and they fitted final drafts into their already overloaded schedules. A big "thank you" to Carolyn Long, Carolyn Thomas, Linda Jenkins, and Susan Dudley.

We want to express a special thanks to our families. Del particularly appreciates the patience of his wife Ruth and children, Amy and Mark. Eugenie is grateful for the support and understanding of her husband Art as well as the patience of their children, Angie, Amy, and Holly.

Appreciation is extended to Guinevera Nance for writing the introduction. Her enthusiasm, support, and encouragement have proven most helpful.

We also thank Gail Hood and Angie Eason for sharing their personal accounts introducing parts of the book. We have changed the names in their stories for the sake of privacy.

A special thanks to Mary Howard for her hours of editing, typing, and re-editing this manuscript. And a hearty thanks to Anne Moore for all her expertise which was needed for the final draft.

TABLE OF CONTENTS

PREFACE

This text is written for older persons who are students or potential students. College recruiters, administrators, and instructors who provide services to these older non-traditional students should also find the content informative. The editors have grouped the chapters into four parts so readers can readily identify areas pertinent to them.

The first part describes returning students, their needs and concerns; the services available on campus to meet their needs; and a review of study skills. By reviewing data gathered through special seminars, a demographic profile of the returning student was developed. This information can aid and encourage older students as it causes them to realize that their situation is typical. They will see that age is not the only similarity they share with others; their needs, concerns, and interests are shared by other older students. They learn how and where to find services and how to study effectively.

The second part identifies specific problems common for the returning student while the third part provides practical coping techniques for addressing problems. Parts II and III discuss special issues facing older students. Some issues (such as abuse and family disruptions) may originate at home while other issues (such as anxiety) may originate at school. Because the chapters are written by different authors, the reader may encounter some overlapping as the authors address various issues and provide specific coping techniques for dealing with impediments to educational progress. The chapters in Part II define some of the relevant problems, such as stress, guilt, and conflicting roles, while Part III is aimed at coping and overcoming these difficulties.

Part IV addresses the concerns of those providing services (administrators) and the instructors of returning students. It is written directly to the administrator, recruiter, and/or class instructor. Chapter 9 addresses educational perspectives, such as special schedules and curriculum changes, which differ for older students. Chapter 10 explains to the instructor, who is in direct contact with the students, how older students differ from traditional students. This chapter offers tips for more effectively teaching these highly motivated students.

The book is written in an easily understood, easy to follow format. The parts are introduced by short but true narratives written by older students. Each story relates to the content of that particular section. We attempted to provide enough information in the table of contents to allow readers to select those parts or chapters most relevant to their personal needs. All suggested readings mentioned are detailed in the appendix.

We ask the reader to remember that the chapters are written by different authors who share their particular expertise. The reader may note differences in structure from chapter to chapter as each author wrote according to their personal style and format. Allowing this literary freedom for the authors may create some content overlap but provides the best and most complete coverage of each topic.

INTRODUCTION

Guinevera A. Nance

There has always been a mystique in America about "going to college"--a phrase that often connotes more than the educational process of classroom lectures, research papers, and final examinations involved in pursuit of a baccalaureate degree. It is a phrase that conjures up visions of bright young men and women settling into dorm rooms or apartments of their own, making new friends as they join fraternities or sororities, pulling "all-nighters" during exam week, and crowding into the stadium on a crisp autumn day to root for the home team. In short, the stereotypic notion of going to college implies a kind of coming of age--a process through which young people gain independence and may learn as much about living as adults as they do the academic subjects in which they major.

The reality of higher education in America is that since the late 1960s increasing numbers of adult students, many of them with family and job responsibilities, have been joining the recent high school graduates on college and university campuses. This trend intensified during the 1970s and 1980s to the point that, in 1977, students 25 years and over in age comprised 38% of the higher education enrollments nationwide and by 1987 accounted for 45% of such enrollments, according to U. S. Department of Education statistics. "Our colleges and universities can never again be described as exclusively the province of the young," noted Fred Harvey Harrington in 1977 in The Future of Adult Education, and that prediction has held beyond the ensuring decade. Projections are that by 1992 the growth in the numbers of non-traditional students (those 25 and over) will have exceeded three

BACK TO SCHOOL AT MY AGE?

million for the two decades, 1972-1992 (Office of Adult Learning Services, The College Board). Already, over five million non-traditional students are enrolled in credit courses.

Thus, today, for nearly half of the students enrolled in institutions of higher education in the United States, "going to college" carries a far different meaning from that contained in the stereotypic picture of academic course work combined with dorm living, frat parties, and football games. For many, it may mean driving across town to an urban campus after work or after the children have been dropped off at school to take one or two courses per academic term (part-time enrollment is largely an adult student phenomenon). It often means juggling the demands of college with those of work and family--perhaps studying for an exam during lunch hours or after everyone else in the house has turned in for the night. For these adult students, who have already come of age socially, the college experience becomes largely a process of growing and developing intellectually.

Because of their maturity and their motivation to learn, non-traditional students often heighten the intellectual seriousness of the undergraduate student body. Intent on making up for lost time, they come to college with an educational purpose--with a desire to learn and a willingness to devote the necessary effort to master new information and ideas. Further, with some "real-world" experience under their belts, they are usually active learners. They question, challenge, and, in general, stimulate the kind of active exchange in the classroom that enlivens learning and that delights most teachers.

My observations about the non-traditional student are gleaned from first-hand experience. I have taught and advised adult students for nearly twenty years at an urban campus that takes pride in its adult population. Also, in the early 1960s, I was what would now be considered a non-traditional student, although the designation of "returning" or "non-traditional" student had yet to come into vogue then. Like most older students, I suspect, I was not so intent on earning a degree when I enrolled in the first evening course (History 101, Western Civilization) as I was on trying out college work and testing myself to see if I were capable of handling it. Also, like many adult students, I was soon hooked on the intellectual excitement of learning despite the cost in time and effort--the rushing home from a full-time job to prepare a quick family dinner and then dashing off to class. For those two hours twice in the evenings each week, I entered what to me was a rarified world--a world of ideas--and gained confidence as I proved my ability to master the work. As I took additional courses and the academic credits mounted up, I began to consider the possibility that one day they might culminate in a degree; but I was wary of thinking too far ahead for fear of being discouraged about the distance left to go. I remember someone asking me how I could stay motivated, plugging along one course at a time. My answer was that I didn't dwell on the amount of academic work left to do, but, instead, concentrated on the work already accomplished. I could not have imagined then that once the baccalaureate degree was completed I would go on to earn a master's and Ph.D., but the perspective of finding encouragement in the progress made rather than despairing over the distance yet to go has proven valuable throughout my career.

It is this lesson that I have tried to impart over the years in working with adult students. In the 1970s, when colleges and universities first began to realize the untapped potential of the 35-and-older college market, the majority of whom were women, I served as academic advisor to a program called Encore. It was designed for women who were returning to college after some hiatus or who were attending college for the first time. It soon became evident that most of these women in their thirties and forties had the ability to do college-level work and, often, to outdo their younger classmates in academic performance. Initially, their confidence was shaky, but it steadied and grew. At times, they momentarily lost heart because the length of the journey to the bachelor's degree seemed so formidable. I remember one of my advisees protesting as I devised a degree plan for her that would lead her to the bachelor's degree in five years of part-time work: "But I'll be forty-five years old when I get my degree." My quick response was a question that shifted her perspective immediately: "And how old will you be in five years if you don't get your degree?" She saw the point and determined that the distanced goal was worth pursuing.

It is out of this belief--that the rewards of higher education for the adult student , however distant they may be, are worth the effort--that this book is written. Intended to encourage those non-traditional students who have already ventured forth into a college curriculum and to prompt adults who may be considering returning to school, <u>Back To School at My Age?</u> offers first-hand experiences of returning students who have successfully navigated through a degree program. This book also contains the valuable insights of educational professionals who have extensive experience in working with non-traditional students. Those of us who have contributed to it do so with the hope that it will be a valuable resource for adults who wish to further their education.

I have on my office wall a plaque that serves to remind me that education is not static, not something one "has" or "acquires," but that it is a process and that new horizons for learning keep opening up throughout our lives. This plaque quotes the twentieth-century philosopher, Will Durant, and says: "Education is the progressive discovery of our ignorance." I like that statement because it reminds me that true education begins when we know that we do not know and are excited about all there is yet to be learned. My wish for the adult students who read this book is that they joyfully discover their ignorance and the excitement of lifelong learning.

PART I

Exploring Motivations, Discovering Services, and Acquiring Skills

The chapters in this part provide useful information to those adults who are considering or who have already committed to continuing their education. You will find discussions addressing issues such as: why return, how to return, and how to be successful.

Chapter 1 is intended to help you analyze your reasons for becoming a returning student. It discusses the general concerns and needs and assists you in relating your unique interests into a "major" area of study. Chapter 2, written by a director of student development, aids you in finding the right school, completing registration, and locating on-campus services. It also provides direct answers to the most frequently asked questions about returning to school.

Chapter 3 places the reader in the classroom. It offers suggestions on where to sit, what to expect, what information you need, etc. It continues with suggestions on how to listen, how to study, how to prepare papers, and how to organize study groups. Utilizing the information in this chapter will help you master the mechanics of learning to ensure your educational goals are reached.

The story in this section is written by a returning student, just like you. It's a first person narrative tracing one person's successful return to school from her initial decision to a satisfying career in education.

Freida's Story

At the age of 27, with two small children, and a low paying secretarial job, I decided to go to college. It sounded simple enough: go to school, become a teacher, earn more money. But my husband and I were barely making ends meet as it was, so how were we going to make it without my income in addition to paying for tuition and books? Looking back, I am not sure how we managed, but we did, and I do not regret any of the struggle during the two and a half years it took to complete my undergraduate degree.

My first quarter in college I took only one night class and still worked full time, so that was not too difficult. Still working full time, I took two night classes my second quarter. After that, I never took less than 20 hours (four classes), and one blurred, consuming quarter I even took 32 hours (seven classes) while still working part time. I continually faced difficulties with money, time, and my family.

Money was a constant problem. The first full year in school I applied for and received a government loan of $500 a quarter. Securing this support wasn't difficult once I initiated the process of obtaining and completing the appropriate forms. This $500 paid for tuition and books with a little left for gas and babysitters. Working part time at odd jobs (secretary, bookkeeper, research assistant, auditor, and cotton surveyor) in the summers supplemented our income. Not only did we have our regular bills to pay, we also had more babysitting charges because I attended school or worked at odd hours of the day and night.

For my second year of school, I applied for and received an academic scholarship. This scholarship was awarded to me by the ROTC program even though I wasn't in ROTC. It only paid for tuition, however, which meant I had to pay for my books. This year was even more difficult than the first, especially when I began student teaching and could no longer work as much.

Time was a commodity I had little of for two years. Because I packed so much into each day, I had no free time at all. I now find it difficult to believe that I survived with my sanity intact. I vividly recall the countless mornings of getting up at 3:00 or 4:00 (before my husband or children would awaken) so I could study or write without distractions. Depending on my class schedule for the quarter, I would either go to work or to school before 8:00 each day and quite often would not return home until after 10:00 at night. Weekends were spent reading, writing, studying, catching up on classwork, and trying to get ahead for the coming week. As an English major, I also spent many long hours in the library researching for papers which were constantly due. Of course, there were still the numerous things that had to be taken care of at home: laundry, dishes, cleaning, and cooking. How many times did I wash and dry clothes at midnight during those two years! My children were young, and my husband did help quite a bit: I certainly appreciated his patience when things weren't done on time.

I know my schooling affected my family, but I hope it was in a more positive than negative way. By necessity, my husband became a wonderful cook and grew closer to the children. He adjusted to doing without things like clean clothes and food until he learned to do them for himself. My daughter was eight years old, my son only five when I began school so they both became more independent. Even today I believe they are more mature than their friends, especially my daughter, as a direct result of having to accept more practical responsibilities. They watched as I studied, listened as I typed, and were quiet as I wrote. When possible, they went with me to the library and even attended several classes. One quarter when I was in a drama production, they regularly attended rehearsals with me and became quite familiar with the campus. Somehow as the years passed, I managed to go to Little League games and to share what free time I had with my family.

Even with all the disadvantages and problems a person with a family may face upon returning to school, the benefits for me as an adult are many. I appreciate my knowledge more and did better in school because I had such a struggle to stay there. I maintained a 2.73 grade point average on a 3.0 scale, remained on the dean's list the entire time I was in school, and graduated with high honors as the most distinguished student in the class. These accomplishments made me feel better about myself: I am a capable individual who can set and achieve goals, even against obstacles that seem impossible. My outlook on life is more positive as I enjoy my belatedly chosen profession, teaching secondary school. Today I often see students struggling to stay in school despite personal problems, and I can readily identify with them. I admire those who stick it out because I know it can be done -- with enough effort, willpower, and determination.

Making a decision, even a right one, that can affect the rest of a person's life is a major step in maturation. It took me longer than some to realize the important consequences of a better education, consequences for both my family and me, but once I did, I saw no reason to delay. Two months before I turned 30, I began teaching in the high school I had attended as a teenager. I earned a master's degree less than four years later and now teach junior college as a second job. Holding down two jobs with a home and two teenage children is not easy, but neither was going to school as an adult. After all, it is never too late to learn, and now I learn something every day because I know I can.

Chapter 1

WHY BE A RETURNING STUDENT?

Del Witherspoon

By picking up this book, you've shown one of two things. Either you are a returning student or you're seriously considering becoming one. Why are you interested in continuing your education? Your answer probably depends on what you want to become and what you hope to have someday. Adults like you are returning to school in significant numbers: many to expand their career possibilities in the hope of improving their financial situation; others for intellectual stimulation and/or for fulfillment of a life-long dream, a college degree.

This chapter has several objectives. It is intended to help you, the older adult, to: better understand why you're returning to school; realize that your needs and concerns are quite normal and can be successfully resolved; and discover and match your interests with an academic area of study.

You are welcome on most college campuses throughout the country. Many universities and colleges allocate resources for recruitment programs and organize retention programs aimed specifically at older students. Many institutions have adjusted to your needs, some more so than others.

Motives

As an adult you have already confronted many of life's realities and have expended considerable energy in searching for your place in the world. You return to campus alert, with determination and with eyes wide open. Getting an education has now become serious business.

Perhaps what brings you back to school is related to a change in your life. It may be a change in your family or a change in your employment. For many, it is a combination of these changes that results in serious self-evaluation. Changes in family may result from a recent death, divorce, or separation. Some use their return to school as a means of coping with family crises. Changes in employment may take you back to school as a necessity. You must be competitive in today's job market. Markus (1973) reported that one-third of surveyed returning students indicated finding the right job as the most important reason for returning to school.

While motives based on financial security or incentives are externally based, there is another basic source of motivation which drives us from within, the desire to achieve. This desire seems to be more enduring than external promises or rewards. For many, this motivation is relentless in that it drives them forward, even against great odds.

Some, like Maslow (1970), feel this internal desire or need to achieve becomes a motivating factor once we have satisfied our more basic needs. If you have already satisfied your social and security needs, your return to school is perhaps to strive for Maslow's highest level of "self-actualization."

Obviously, for most students internal and external motives account for their persistent efforts to return to and remain in school. In Frieda's story, it is obvious she pursued a better life for her family, but as an old friend, I attest to her intense desire to achieve and to become a better human being.

As an adult, you have become more cautious as you plot the course of your future. You have a desire to succeed but, at the same time, you're concerned about possible failure. Returning students routinely ask such questions as, "Why? Why am I here?", "Do I need this?", and "Can I accomplish this?".

If you're like most returning students, you wish to grow personally and to be successful in both your family and career as well as satisfy your basic need to achieve. You want to give your loved ones all they deserve, both educational advantages and other opportunities. You want to do this, however, with style and in a career which you enjoy.

Primarily your success on campus is up to you. Maybe Maslow is correct as it appears to be human nature to strive for achievement. "Self" awareness and a desire to become a better "self" are both part of the struggle to grow as a person. It seems to be natural for us to go for that which is barely within our grasp and to strive for that just beyond our reach. As free individuals, we differ as to how we strive for achievement and in what areas we strive. Our levels of motivation vary and our goal may be only a fleeting thought for others. Regardless of the reasons for returning to school, older students are seeking a brighter future.

As yesterday's careers quickly become obsolete, your commitment to a career that will provide financial security becomes extremely important. Your job may have been a casualty of the rapidly changing economy. For some of your co-workers, it is the end of the road. They will never attempt new training. Others will try but won't succeed. Many displaced workers need special support programs to identify and validate choices. Often older individuals experience physical and emotional changes which coincide with a forced job or career change. This combination may prove devastating to an already fragile self-image. Hearing your child say "my mom or dad goes to school" is not a boost to an already diminished level of confidence. Rather than interpreting a career change as a consequence of a poor decision, you must expect and accept "change" as a routine part of your career. Willingly accepting change increases the potential for success which, in our culture, is too often equated with income.

It is better to be propelled by desire to achieve than handicapped by the fear of failure. For example, let's say your employer has become interested in your progress. He's started paying your tuition and giving you some time off to study and attend class. Though you may have initially considered his interest supportive, you may come to fear that failure could jeopardize your job or your credibility on the job. The fear of failure can easily negate the confidence you have gained from successful job performance or completion of earlier courses. You must let the satisfaction derived from small achievements (each exam or paper) serve as a personal reward for positive growth and not to build a barrier to prevent failure or avoid ridicule. Don't allow fear of failure to become the motivational force for your educational achievements.

You may not be seeking a college degree but desire practical knowledge to enhance your performance as an employee, parent, spouse, and/or friend. For others, completing a college education may be a dream for retirement years. Whatever the individual motivation, if you have a genuine desire and are persistent, you can achieve your educational goals. Regardless of your motivation, from whatever source, you mustn't turn back. Retreat would burden you with remorse, such as "I should have. . ." "I missed my chance," "It's just too late," or "If only."

Specific Needs and Concerns

Recently a study at Auburn University at Montgomery (Jenkins & Witherspoon, 1991) focused on the interests and concerns of older students. These students were polled at "returning to school" seminars which were attended on a voluntary basis by older students. When asked about intended majors, both females and males overwhelmingly indicated business with management, accounting, and finance as common specialties. There was also interest in science, liberal arts, and education. Females often indicated nursing also.

This same study revealed personal concerns of males and females. Inability to finance education was the main concern reported by females who also expressed concerns about taking tests, family matters, and general coping with school. Remarks such as "need advice" reflected concerns of women. With only a few concerned about finances, men were most concerned about transfer credits.

Roehl (1981) found women who returned to school were happier, healthier, and more interested in life. For the past two decades more females have returned to school. Exceptions have been those periods immediately following major military conflicts, such as Vietnam when, just as after World War II and the Korean Conflict, returning students were males in their mid to late 20s who attended under the GI Bill. Today the average age of both female and male returning students is close to 35. The typical returning student is a married woman with two children, perhaps teenagers, and whose husband holds a top level job (Scott, 1980).

With today's economy, males frequently find they can no longer be the family's sole breadwinner. More and more families have determined that both men and women must share the role of provider to meet the family's needs. With more women in the job market, the male is often called upon to be a more active, involved parent. Having grown up in an era when the father's primary responsibility was his career, today's fathers have few role models for fulfilling their expanding parental responsibilities. Meeting the demands of several roles as well as being a student can prove quite difficult. The university may be wise to offer guidance and support to those students attempting to fulfill multiple roles. Chapter 4 discusses this issue in more detail.

Domestic and child care responsibilities are culturally embedded in the mother. She has traditionally assumed responsibility for basically raising the children, arranging for their transportation and child care. On-campus child care can be a most welcome resource for mothers who return to college.

Mangano and Corrado (1980) conducted a survey on the special needs of adult students. Their survey revealed several high priority needs relating to administrative policies. Needs included: courses that develop specific employment skills; availability of evening classes; and credits for life experiences. In the area of instructional patterns, the surveys indicated that returning students rate as most important instructors who: are interested in their progress; are relaxed and friendly; use realistic examples; and are cognizant of responsibilities outside of class.

From time to time, you may be concerned about intellectual ability, financial support, or family support. Worries about the future are magnified for most older students. Having already faced life's uncertainties, these doubts, concerns, and worries are tempered by mature realism. Just a little effort by the university to provide adequate information can reap benefits for returning students and the university. For you, a returning student, education is an important undertaking and its cost is much more than financial as time and energy have now become treasured resources.

Obviously you have different needs and concerns from those of more traditional students. You need understanding from both the administration and the faculty. Special services and consideration in scheduling classes are important to your segment of the campus population.

Perhaps these comments echo some of your needs and concerns. Also, as an older student, male or female, the pressure to justify your re-entry into the educational system and declare a specific major is intense. Before making this decision, however, we want you to take a little time to survey your interests to discover those that most closely relate to a specific academic major.

Declaring a Major

According to Chickering (1969), students are searching for academic purpose. Choosing an area of study, both major and minor, is important in providing purpose, goals, and self-direction. Whether from home or from the educational sector, intentionally or unintentionally, those providing the financial resources apply pressure for degree decisions. This pressure may create additional anxiety resulting in decisions too hastily made without necessary information. With unanswered questions about career opportunities or requirements, frustration and/or conflict is inevitable.

Yes, setting goals is important. If your goal is a college degree, you shouldn't wait until you decide on a major (special area of study) to enroll. When asked to declare a major, you're not being asked to chisel it in stone. Majors can be changed or modified to reflect changing interests as more information is acquired. You should attempt to understand and transform your interests into reasonable career goals. Interests change just as national economics and career opportunities change. Many required courses, such as introduction to psychology or sociology, are designed to familiarize students with different areas.

You may find that analyzing your personal interests is not an easy task. Often the image, income level, and/or title of a particular career appear attractive; however, the price for success in that field may require more than meets the eye. Having to study material you do not find interesting may prove difficult and result in poor performance and grades unacceptable for degree requirements. Marginal grades can damage self-confidence, deflate your self-image, and discourage further efforts. Sometimes such a failure is not the result of a lack of ability but a result of a lack of genuine interest because of a poor choice.

Understanding personal assets and deficits can be an extra plus when selecting a career. For example, if you thrive on locating and correcting small details, you may become an excellent accountant or computer programmer. If getting "close" is good enough and you want to move on to other things, you probably would not be happy nor successful in these fields. If you truly enjoy people, you may prefer business, especially sales and management. If you want to influence others' lives, you may prefer education or the social sciences, perhaps working as a teacher, psychologist, counselor, or social worker.

Older students enjoy the advantage of having already been a part of the "real" world. You will soon realize that your life experiences can be a distinct advantage. Much general knowledge is acquired through raising children, working, and reading. These experiences provide insight and understanding into otherwise dull theories, thus making learning more meaningful and easier to integrate into your existing core of knowledge. Personal ideas about available and desirable career opportunities have begun to develop; however, doubts linger about correct choices, especially when several areas seem equally interesting and appealing.

One useful technique for assessing interests is to acknowledge how much free time is spent reading material in a specific area. Reading geology, psychology, business trends, management techniques, health, history, etc. reflects a genuine interest in that area. You may find you have several such interests which should be seriously considered as a possible major or minors. These areas of interest should be explored for potential employment possibilities. There are career offices on most campuses to provide information on current career opportunities. Industry communicates regularly with these offices concerning their needs and specific employment requirements. Your local library should have several publications evaluating the current status and potential of careers. An excellent source would be the Occupational Outlook Handbook published annually by the Department of Labor.

There are several tests, such as the Strong Interest Inventory, for evaluating interests and suitability for specific careers. results can usually be assessed during an interview with a qualified career counselor. Most institutions provide this service to potential students.

Another convenient and practical way to discover preferences is to scan the prospective school's catalog. This may lead you to a general area of study. There are basically four general areas of studies: science, education, business, and liberal arts. Some schools expand these areas to include fields such as aviation, pharmacy, engineering, agriculture, and nursing. Many institutions offer post-graduate degrees in the areas mentioned above as well as in law, medicine, and veterinary medicine.

Each of the four general areas is composed of a number of specialty areas. Each specialty is controlled by an individual department within the university. For example, the science area or "school" offers majors in biology, physics, math, psychology, etc.

Confusing? Really it's much easier than it may appear. Many specialties overlap and blend together. For example, if you are interested in both education and psychology or education and biology, you may elect to teach psychology or biology. If you like both psychology and business, you might consider personnel management, organizational behavior, or industrial psychology.

Perhaps you now understand why your interests don't have to be too focused; you are not limited to one area or major. Your minor or minors can include other interests. Though you may not be aware of it, you can get degrees in several majors if you want or you can have more than a single minor. While remembering that majors can be changed by a simple process, you should realize that additional credit hours may be needed to meet requirements for a different major. This is particularly noteworthy the closer you are to graduation.

As you register, it is advisable to declare a major area of study, ask for an advisor, and schedule a meeting with the advisor to discuss your goals. The advisor will monitor your educational progress.

The AUM study referred to earlier (Jenkins & Witherspoon, 1991) revealed that those who declared a major early in their return to school and took more hours their first quarter were most likely to graduate. Also, more degrees were earned in business than other fields.

Equating success with income may explain why both older and younger students are declaring business as their major. A 1989 report by the Scientific Research Society presented data showing an increase in overall college freshmen who expressed interest in business careers. The data reflect a declining interest in educational and scientific careers. While the enrollment of men in business courses has increased, women's enrollment in business has increased even more rapidly. Based on this survey, the reasons for attending college were more for earning money than for education itself. Earning money was more important in 1988 than in 1976. While earning potential was the main reason reported by those entering business schools, income was not nearly as important for those selecting humanities and arts, biological sciences, and social sciences.

Those pursuing a business major need to focus on specific areas and bring more than just general business knowledge to a potential employer. Teachers, especially those with scientific specialties, continue to be in demand. Some fields of study, such as psychology and sociology, offer most potential at the master or doctorate levels, although graduates with bachelor degrees may find employment in public institutions and agencies. With a continuing shortage, nursing remains a viable field as does medical technology.

In summary, we hope this chapter has helped you to better understand why you have returned to school or why you want to return. By acknowledging your needs and concerns, we want you to recognize yourself as a very special, understood, and welcome student on today's college campus. Universities and colleges are eager to accept you, are aware of your concerns, and understand your uncertainties. (You may find comfort in knowing that your concerns are justified and are shared by many and have been concerns of students before you.) Setting goals, determining interests, declaring a major, utilizing an advisor, and exploring all available options are all encouraged and are to your advantage.

Although dreams can soar to great heights, many small steps or achievements are necessary to reach those heights. Weekly and daily accomplishments serve as stepping stones to ultimate goals. Every exam taken, every chapter read, and every paper completed are minor achievements that should be savored with satisfaction and garnished with pride.

Your educational goal, whether a Ph.D., a two year associate degree, or only a few completed courses, is an investment in yourself. Educational accomplishments are personal marketable improvements in yourself that no one can take from you. They require drive, initiative, and determined action on your part. Inquiry begins the process, a process that must be begun if you are to earn that degree!

References

Chickering, A. W. (1980) Education and Identity. San Francisco: Jossey-Bass.

Jenkins, L. and Witherspoon, A. (1991). Assessment of Interests, Needs, and Concerns of Returning Students Attending Recruitment Programs. Unpublished manuscript. Auburn University at Montgomery.

Levinson, D. J. (1977). The Mid-Life Transition: A Period in Adult Psychosocial Development. Psychiatry, 40, 99-112.

Mangano, J. and Corrado, T. (1980). Adult Student Needs. NASPA Forum, 1 (1), as cited in Midstate ACT as a strategic resource in meeting student and institutional needs, 1988-89, 2.130-2.131.

Markus, H. (1973). Continuing education for women: Factors influencing a return to school and the school experience (Report No. AC 014-489). Ann Arbor: University of Michigan.

Maslow, A. H. (1970). Motivation and Personality (2nd ed.) New York: Harper & Row.

Roehl, J. E. (1981). Stressful life events of reentry women students (Doctoral dissertation, Arizona State University, 1980). Dissertation Abstracts International, 42, 505A.

Scott, N. A. (1980). Returning women students: A review of research and descriptive studies. Washington, D. C.: National Association for Women Deans, Administrators and Counselors.

Contrary to what you may have heard, all colleges want the students they accept to be successful. Most colleges provide services to assist students with many of the challenges they will face. A good place to begin to discover available student services is at new student orientation or in the student handbook. If you are not given a handbook when you enroll, ask for one. Some information about services is also in the college catalog.

Typical services offered to all students include guidance through admission and registration, financial aid, tutoring, job placement, career counseling, and personal counseling services. Some colleges also offer an office of returning student services. These offices may provide anything from academic advice to free coffee for tired commuters.

Selecting a School

How do you gather the information you need to make that initial decision to begin or continue your education? First, you need to check all the higher education options available within the geographical area you decide is appropriate for you. Local chambers of commerce provide lists of all higher education institutions, their addresses, and telephone numbers.

Be aware that all institutions with the word "college" in the name are not necessarily accredited institutions of higher education. They may not offer courses which will transfer to another institution or lead to a degree. These schools may offer programs which are attractive to you; however, be sure you understand the kind and extent of training offered. Schools with "college" in the name can include proprietary schools, junior, technical, or community colleges, as well as private and public institutions which offer at least a four-year degree. If a school is accredited, it has met established minimum standards judged as important by other institutions of higher education and/or professional organizations.

Proprietary schools are established to make a profit for the owners. Just as with other kinds of educational institutions, the

Chapter 2

EXTENDING A HAND: SUPPORT PROGRAMS

Linda R. Jenkins

Did you drop out of school to get married? Are you a successful business person who never completed that college degree? Are you looking for personal enrichment or professional advancement?

Whatever your personal history, you have probably thought about going to college -- either for the first time or after an extended absence from formal education. If you are like most adults thinking about entering those hallowed halls of academe, you have more questions than answers, and many of those questions aren't answered in the correspondence provided by the college admissions office.

In your higher education adventure, the first step, finding answers to these questions, is often the most difficult. Even adults who have some college experience are intimidated by the higher education system of admissions tests, credits, and prerequisites. It is even more difficult for those who have no prior college. Those of us who work in higher education often forget that the jargon we use may be an obstacle to those who aren't familiar with our terms. It is helpful to remember our own confusion when the mechanic explains in detail just what made our car die.

quality of the programs as well as the costs in proprietary schools will vary.

Generally, technical colleges offer training toward a specific skilled area such as air conditioning and heating, auto mechanics, or office management. These programs may offer courses in English and job related mathematics; however, seldom do these courses count as college credit. This may be because the course length does not equal the time spent in a typical college class, the instructor may lack minimum qualifications for college teaching, or the instruction may be job specific.

Junior and community colleges offer two year programs that may lead either to an associate degree or certification in a particular area. Usually courses taken at a junior or community college may be transferred to a four year institution; however, each college has its own standards so you must check with the institution to which you wish to transfer for specific advice about transfer requirements.

Private colleges and universities range from very small and relatively unknown institutions to well-known, prestigious universities. Programs, costs, and admission requirements vary.

Public colleges and universities receive funding from the state and vary in size and tuition as well. They also vary in the programs and services and in requirements for admission.

For this discussion, the term "college" will refer to public and private institutions of higher education which offer at least a bachelor's degree (a four year degree).

When you have the names and addresses of colleges in your geographic location, begin to gather additional information from each. Usually the admissions office is the first place to contact. Some smaller schools may combine the admissions office with an another administrative office like financial aid or the office of the registrar; however, every college will have someone designated to answer questions related to admission requirements. Whether you write or call for information, be sure you request a copy of the most recent catalog, an application for admission, and any other specific information of interest to you. For example, you may also want to know about scholarships available.

The interesting work begins when you receive the information from the college. As you read this information, keep a pencil handy to mark those areas about which you have questions. Sometimes you will find the answers to your questions a little further in the printed material; if not, ask someone for clarification. Providing the most comprehensive information, the college catalog explains what the college provides as well as what responsibilities belong to the student.

There is a definite skill in asking the right questions of college personnel. Just as in any business endeavor, colleges hire new personnel and experienced staff are away from work from time to time. You may not get all the information you need on your first call to the college. Be patient but persistent in your efforts to have your questions answered.

When you are considering colleges, some things to question are the academic programs offered, admission requirements, class times, costs, amount and kind of academic counseling available, and campus services such as financial aid, tutoring, job placement, and child care.

Approaching The Admissions and Registrar's Office

After you have read all the material, it is time to talk to advisors in the admissions office at the schools that interest you. It is always best to call for an appointment so that you will be sure to have the undivided attention of the counselor. When you call for an appointment, be sure to ask if there is a counselor who specializes in advising adult students. Even if there are no counselors designated just for returning students, there are often individuals who are especially attuned to the needs of returning students. Some of the counselors were returning students themselves and will offer encouragement and support.

Frequently adults are hesitant to talk to academic advisors because they are undecided about an area of study, or "major" as it's called in college jargon. They are embarrassed because they haven't decided what they want to be when they "grow up." Although some adults have definite ideas about what they want to study as well as when and how they want to do it, it is not at all unusual for adult students to want to try a little of everything before they decide on a major.

Personnel in the admissions office will help you with the admissions process. You must complete an application for admission and have official copies of transcripts from all colleges you have attended sent to the admissions office. If you have never attended college, you must have a copy of your high school transcript sent to the college. It doesn't matter how long you have been out of high school, a record of your graduation will be on file. There are situations, however, which are unusual. If your school has merged with another or if records have been destroyed in a fire or similar disaster, the counselor will explain the college's policy for handling special situations.

You may also be required to take a college entrance examination like the American College Test (ACT) or Scholastic Aptitude Test (SAT). Adults are often afraid to take these tests; however, there are ways to prepare yourself, limit your test anxiety, and improve your score. Study guides are available which acquaint you with the subject area and types of questions on the test. Some colleges even offer short courses to prepare prospective students to take the test.

Ask if the college you plan to attend offers a special classification category for returning students. Some colleges have categories which allow returning students to be admitted conditionally before they take entrance examinations. Other colleges may omit the test requirements entirely. If you are admitted conditionally, there are usually additional requirements you must satisfy before you will be fully admitted to the college.

The admission process may be more stressful in some colleges than others. You may begin to feel that there is always one more hoop to jump through before you can be fully accepted to the college. There are usually good reasons for the requirements, but if you wonder about these reasons, ask someone. A sincere question asked without malice will usually be answered with patience and understanding. It may also provide you with more insight into the college and its goals for its students.

If you have no prior college experience, you will be advised to take courses in the "core curriculum," general education requirements for all students which provides a common background for all areas of study. The core curriculum usually includes courses in English composition, history, natural or physical sciences, mathematics, and general electives. Electives allow you to sample courses in different departments and may help you identify areas of interest for your major. Every college determines its own core curriculum, so don't be distressed if you completed American history at a college you attended years ago and now learn that the college you want to attend requires world history.

If you have college credits from other schools, your transcripts will be evaluated and you will be told which courses will count toward your degree. Sometimes this evaluation is done in the admissions office and sometimes it is done elsewhere on campus. No matter who does the evaluation, you should be provided a form or statement explaining exactly what will apply toward your degree. Be sure to keep this statement for future reference.

Financial Aid: Loans, Grants, and Scholarships

Many returning students assume that they will not be eligible for any kind of financial assistance because they or their spouse work full time, so they don't bother to apply. Most colleges offer both need-based and merit-based forms of financial assistance.

Need-based assistance includes federal and state funded grants, loans, jobs, and scholarships. To apply, students must complete federally approved need analysis documents detailing information from tax returns, data about financial assets, and family size. This information is used to determine how much the student can be expected to contribute toward his or her educational expenses. Though the forms are admittedly complicated, every college has professional staff to help with them. It should never be necessary to pay someone to help you apply for financial aid.

Merit-based financial assistance is awarded for exceptional talent or achievement in a particular area. Academic scholarships are usually awarded to students on the basis of their demonstrated achievement in the classroom. Returning students are often exceptional students whose grades make them excellent candidates for academic scholarships. On most campuses you won't be given a scholarship, no matter how good your grades are, unless you apply for it. Ask about application deadlines and complete the application process.

Some colleges require scholarship recipients to be full time students. Full time is generally defined as being enrolled for a minimum of 12 hours. With other responsibilities, returning students may attend only part time. If scholarships are not available to part time students, question the reasons for this policy. It may be possible to designate some scholarships for returning students.

Financial assistance may be available from your employer or from organizations in your community. Some employers reimburse employees for part or all of their tuition if they maintain certain grades and/or take courses which will improve job skills. This is definitely a possibility worth checking into.

You may be a member of an organization that promotes continuing education for its members by offering scholarships and grants. Even a small amount of money can make a difference to returning students on a tight budget. There is also the intangible reward that students receive from knowing someone supports them in their academic endeavors.

It may also be financially beneficial to check with the office that receives your tuition payments to see if alternate payment plans are available. Some colleges require that all tuition be paid before you are allowed to attend class; others allow you to pay tuition in installments. This service may be available but not publicized, so ask if you are interested.

Other Services and Campus Life

Tutoring is a service returning students may avoid because they see it as an admission of weakness. In reality, even better students often request tutoring. In addition to improving certain skills needed for success in the classroom, tutoring can build your confidence in all subjects.

Many colleges have a central tutoring service (sometimes called a learning or skills center) while others offer tutoring through individual departments. Workshops may be offered to develop study skills, relieve test anxiety, and offer suggestions for taking essay or multiple choice tests. If information is not readily available about this service, keep asking. If it isn't being offered, it should be -- and your persistence may help make it a reality.

Returning students often have to balance their academic responsibilities with family obligations and job requirements. There is always stress on students to perform at maximum capacity in all areas. The stress may be applied by others, but many times, returning students put pressure on themselves. Most colleges have professional counselors to help students deal with the everyday pressures associated with attending college. For the traditional student, the pressure may be related to roommate problems. For the returning student, the stress may also be roommate related -- the roommate may just be the student's spouse. Students should not hesitate to use professional counseling services. The services are usually free or available for a nominal fee, and they may keep a small problem from growing into a situation that threatens academic success.

As in any counseling situation, college counseling centers adhere to the strictest standards of confidentiality. If you are unsure about the credentials of counselors, ask the director of the center to tell you about the credentials of the staff. Just as you will find in other areas, there are probably some counselors who were returning students themselves who will understand your concerns.

Why would returning students who already have busy schedules want to add to their overload by participating in campus life? Perhaps because the advantages are as valuable to them as they are to the traditional students.

Most colleges have student clubs and honor societies related to each field of study. Participation in these organizations helps students get to know other students and faculty who share their interests. These small groups form the basis for informal study groups and lasting friendships. They also help students develop a sense of belonging on campus. Students who feel like they belong are much more likely to seek help when it is needed and to stay in school until they reach their goal.

There are other activities which can provide a free or inexpensive connection to the college as well as entertainment for returning students. Lectures, movies, theater performances, and athletic events are just some of the activities offered by most colleges. An added advantage to participating in such events with family members is that it involves them in your academic adventure.

Support Systems

A good support system is a valuable asset to any student but is particularly important to returning students. Before you begin class, take stock of your personal support system. You may have a spouse who takes pride in your decision to return to college and volunteers to take on an extra share of family responsibilities. Your children may enjoy watching you study and may even decide to compete with you for good grades. Your employer may notice your initiative and reward you with positive comments about your decision. Even better, you may be offered a flexible work schedule to help you during peak study times.

Parents may be so glad that you have decided to attend college that they offer to provide child care or pay a portion of your tuition.

Self Analysis

Some self analysis may ease the transition between your old life and that of a college student. Read the following questions and answer them honestly to yourself. Your chances of successfully achieving your educational goals are enhanced by affirmative answers. However, don't let negative responses discourage you. The questions that you truthfully respond to negatively are only indicative of areas you need to focus on changing to ensure success.

Is your educational goal self chosen?

Your goal should be chosen by you for you, not to satisfy the goals others may have set for you. If your educational goal is actually your parents' or wife's goal, you may find their goal difficult to achieve.

Does your goal involve some risks?

Your goal should provide you a challenge, thereby presenting risks or the possibility of failure. Some degree of risk results in greater gratification when steps toward a challenging goal are accomplished.

Have you divided your ultimate goal into smaller steps or sub-goals?

Dividing ultimate goals into basic components is an aggressive technique. As you approach these sub-goals, sub-divide them into even smaller steps. For example, this quarter your psychology course includes two papers, three tests, and one book review. Each of these course requirements is a small component in the larger goal of passing psychology which is a step in attaining the ultimate goal, your degree.

Do you expect to succeed?

Your expectations are very important. Studying for an exam with the expectation of passing provides confidence. Expecting failure creates interfering anxiety and additional confusion.

Can you engage in self-criticism?

Self-criticism is a healthy way for personal growth. Taking inventory or becoming aware of your weaknesses allows you to focus on areas needing development, for example writing skills.

Are you willing to ask questions, seek and consult various resources?

When studying material that is not clear, you should not hesitate to ask for clarification. It may very well be the material was not presented in a clear, complete manner and needs further explanation. Usually questions help you as well as the instructor and other students. Be willing to seek answers from available resources. Today, through extensive computer networks and library loan programs, resources are practically limitless.

Do you daydream and imagine your success?

Allow yourself to daydream, but, of course, not during lectures or study periods. Daydreaming frequently produces innovative ideas as well as encouragement for persisting. Imagine yourself at graduation or accepting the job you want. While it is healthy to daydream, discipline your study habits so your dreams will become reality.

Though you may feel alone in facing the dilemma of returning to school, this is not true. Many older, non-traditional students have paved the way for you. They began with many of the same concerns you now have. A few frequently asked questions and their responses are presented below:

Q.   Can I compete with the younger students in demanding courses like algebra, English, or history?

A.   Usually these doubts are laid to rest after successfully completing one or two courses. Patience and persistence are required to increase skills in math, speaking, writing, and critical thought.

Q.   Do I have what it takes to get a college degree?

A.   Failure or dropping out is more of a product of stress than a lack of ability. Positive expectations and optimism will propel you toward success.

Q.   How can I ever reach such a distant goal -- a degree four years or more in the future?

A.   Plan and dream big, but think in terms of the small steps or increments necessary to achieve that goal. Hang a graph on the wall charting your progress.

Q.   How do I enroll?

A.   Just pick up the telephone and call the admissions office or the university operator. Or better yet, find the office, open the door and walk in; they are waiting to help you.

Q.   How will younger students react to my presence?

A.   The older student is now an integral part of the classroom. With non-traditional students comprising 30-50% of today's enrollment, you will not be an unusual sight.

Q.   Will I be comfortable in the classroom; will my comments or experiences be relevant?

A.   Certainly there will be some apprehension at first, but it will quickly change to comfort and confidence. Your life experiences can be valuable to other students and the instructor. You can provide realism and applicability to otherwise vague, academic theories.

Q.   What are my expectations for utilizing my degree; are they reasonable?

A.   This is a problem when programs are oversold. Talking to those working in the type job you want will help you discern the realities of today's job market. Do not rely solely on university staff; talk with professionals in your career field.

Q.   Where can I go for support or help?

A.   Your instructor or advisor can direct you to the appropriate personnel. Most universities provide counseling centers, tutoring and learning centers, financial aid advisors, and returning student organizations.

Q.   Can I get credit for my job experiences and training?

A.   Some schools allow credits for career experiences. Most will allow elective credits for military training; others may allow you to "challenge" a course by testing-out of the class. This is worth discussing with your advisor.

Q.   What are CLEP credits?

A.   Many universities recognize these national exams and will give you credit for having completed requirements for these courses if you pass the written examination. This is an excellent way to quickly pass the basic first year courses such as history, English, and math.

Q.   How do I find an advisor?

A.   Early contact with an advisor is important. While some schools may assign you an advisor, some schools may leave the selection of an advisor up to you. Select an advisor in the department of your major and contact him/her as soon as possible. You can always change advisors later if necessary.

Q.   Will my grade point average (GPA) be affected by earlier, perhaps less serious, attempts at school?

A.   Earlier grades can affect your acceptance into academic programs. Even when courses are retaken, the first grade usually remains on the transcript. Some schools are beginning to offer an academic bankruptcy policy which allows students to be "forgiven" for a limited number of unseccessful attempts in the classroom. This policy if available, will vary from one institution to another.

Q.   What is a residency requirement?

A.   You must establish credibility at the university or college which will award you the degree. Usually you are required to attend classes your last year or 45 hours.

Q.   Will a college degree make me successful?

A.   You probably have several definitions of success -- happiness, wealth, etc. Usually education is linked to financial success.   However, there is more involved in success than your gross salary. To be successful financially, you must learn to handle complex financial decisions.   A college degree does not come with a guaranteed salary nor with the financial expertise to make sound financial decisions.   The non-credit condensed courses offered by your university's continuing education program are a practical source of information for developing financial skills.

Summary

This chapter should be very helpful if you've never attended college or if your earlier attempt was a brief, half-hearted effort. Knowing what services are available and how to locate and utilize them is to your advantage. Use them, they are there for you.

Every student's situation is different. Analyze your situation and take advantage of your particular strengths. Students do manage to have a successful college experience when there are no obvious support systems in place. Determination and creativity are essential ingredients for success in these situations. How can you make it through college when the odds are against you?

*Decide that you want a college education.

*Prepare yourself. Identify your academic strengths and weaknesses and begin to work on your weaknesses.

*Gather information. Learn everything you can about the colleges in your area.

*Utilize the resources that are available to you. Public libraries, high school counselors, church support groups, and individual college offices are some examples of free resources.

*Find others who share your interest in learning. You won't be the only returning student on campus. Sharing your concerns with someone in a similar situation may help both of you.

*Ask for help when you need it. Wise students don't wait until the end of the term to ask the professor for help. Most professors keep regular office hours and will be happy to schedule an appointment with you.

*Assert yourself. If your college is not responsive to the needs of returning students, let them hear from you. If you offer reasonable alternatives in a rational manner, you can make a difference for all returning students. Be prepared to submit your requests in writing and be willing to go through channels. Nothing changes rapidly in higher education.

*Accept something less than perfection. It's wonderful to make an "A", but there is life after a "B" or a "C". You have to make choices and sometimes it just isn't possible to do everything perfectly. You do not have to make perfect grades, be a perfect spouse, parent, and employee all at the same time.

Chapter 3

LEARNING TO LEARN

Del Witherspoon

For some, assimilating new knowledge seems to be natural, fairly easy, or even fun. If you are such a person, you probably owe your good fortune to someone, a parent or teacher, who taught you a few basic learning skills. You may have observed the haphazard approach taken by others and been amazed at how they made a simple task difficult, frustrating, and defeating.

If you have never learned some basic do's and don'ts about studying effectively and efficiently, you will find the information in this chapter both interesting and beneficial. As an older student, you probably have more than your share of distractions and off-campus responsibilities, responsibilities that are, in fact, more important than the course you've enrolled in recently. Job, family, and elderly parents are all high priorities on your daily agenda. Increasing your studying proficiency can be time saving, stress reducing, and perhaps even remove some guilt. For example, wouldn't you be pleased to study less but earn even better grades? Would you like to complete study requirements quicker and have more time for family? How about cutting your studying time in half while improving your grade point average? Sound good? This chapter will teach you how to do just that.

For your convenience, we've divided this material into eight parts. Select those which you feel will help you the most and then modify your study habits to suit your needs.

Orientation to the Setting

Obtaining answers to questions concerning each particular college enables you to select the college of your choice. Its curriculum and reputation, based on comments from those who are attending or who have previously attended, can be helpful. After utilizing Chapter 2 in selecting the institution best suited to you and in proceeding through the admission and registration processes, you are now ready to acclimate yourself to your campus.

Walk around the campus. Locate tutoring services, counseling services, drink machines, smoking areas, possible study areas, and your classrooms. Once you're familiar with your surroundings, it will be much easier to relax and study.

When it's time to go to class, arrive early and sit where you feel the most comfortable. Usually the seat you take for the first class period becomes "your" seat for the remainder of the course. Occasionally the instructor may require a special seating arrangement, but this is rare on a college campus. Sit where you can hear well as all college instructors are not great speakers. You will find that most instructors are intelligent people dedicated to sharing specific information about their expertise, but their sharing is not necessarily in the most effective manner.

As a returning student, you may be older than the instructor. If you attend a university, you may be surprised to have a graduate student teaching the course. This teacher, called a graduate teaching assistant, may be pursuing a master's or doctorate degree and be satisfying a requirement by teaching freshman courses. Normally there is a professor responsible for the class, but you rarely see him or her once the graduate teaching assistant has demonstrated proficiency. Though you thought you would be the only apprehensive person in the classroom, this young teacher may appear uncomfortable or apprehensive also. By being supportive and friendly, you may alleviate your own apprehension as well as the teacher's!

Another possibility is that you will encounter a teacher whom you just don't like. You have the option of dropping the class and picking up another. "Dropping" or "adding" courses is usually allowed during the first week of classes. Don't be too hasty, though. Adjusting to this instructor can be educational in itself. Ask other students before you change classes. Your first impression may prove totally wrong.

Normally, you will receive an outline of the course, or syllabus, during the first class period. It provides you with specific reading requirements and dates of particular lectures, exams, and completion of papers. It should also explain how grades are calculated. For example, two exams during the quarter may combine to count as 50% of the course grade, a special paper 10%, and the final exam 40%. Ask questions such as: What type of test questions will be used? True/False? Multiple choice? Matching? Discussion? Is the final exam comprehensive? How much of the exam will be comprehensive, 40%, 60%, etc.?

By getting answers to these questions, you know what to expect which can be instrumental in putting you at ease. Usually more seasoned students ask relevant questions such as: What is the attendance policy? Are there make-up exams? Will there be take home tests? What are the instructor's office hours and where is the office? Is there a special assistance area with tutors and computers in this department? Are you allowed to ask questions during lectures or must you wait until after the lecture?

What if the instructor doesn't show up for class? Generally, after waiting 10 to 15 minutes and receiving no instructions from the instructor, you are free to leave or you may stay and study. This does not happen often but once in a while an instructor has an accident or sudden illness.

This sort of information is gained primarily through osmosis as you attend classes. It seems to be assumed that everyone knows all the ins and outs of college life, but minor details like those mentioned above are frustrating for new or returning students.

Factors Affecting Learning

Probably the major factor affecting learning is an individual's level of motivation. Your motivation may come from within, such as a desire to learn and understand yourself. This motivation acts like an enduring push or drive. On the other hand, your motivation may be from without, an incentive such as degree or the money it may enable you to earn. This type of motivation appears to pull you along quarter by quarter. Both motivational factors are enhanced if you establish goals. Hopefully, chapters 1 and 2 helped you identify and set personal goals which are attainable as well as challenging. Regardless of your motivation, setting unreasonable goals may result in setbacks, failures, frustrations, loss of interest, and diminished motivation.

Other important factors that affect learning include: (1) how the material is presented in the text or by the lecturer; (2) how much time you study and review the material; (3) the quality of the study time or your studying techniques; (4) how much and how quickly you're provided feedback from your test answers; (5) how meaningful the material is for you; and (6) how interesting and rewarding your work is for you.

The first three of the factors are closely related. The method of presentation greatly impacts initial retention. You retain much more when you see and hear information rather than merely hearing it. You retain even more if you are allowed to participate and review the material, say in a class discussion. You may want to devote part of your study time to participating in small study groups where you can rehearse and review information together. The value received from your studying, reviewing, and rehearsing is dependent upon how well you utilize time. Breaking study time into segments will result in greater learning. For example, it seems better to study four one hour periods during the day than to sit and study continuously for one long four hour stretch.

Techniques for improving the quality of your study time are presented throughout this chapter.

The fourth factor, how quickly you're provided feedback, is important in learning. Your learning process is hindered if you respond but then it's two weeks before you're told whether your response was correct. If the instructor is slow in returning test papers, it makes learning more difficult. Though some instructors view exams as only a means to acquire an evaluation score, exams themselves can be an excellent teaching tool. Immediately following an exam period, take time to research answers to questions you weren't sure about.

Another variable directly related to how well and quickly you learn is the "meaningfulness" of the material. Courses outside your major area of study may initially seem boring and tedious. Your studies may be interrupted by recurring thoughts such as, "Why do I need this? I'm not going to be a historian or journalist." While some of these thoughts may be justified, you must remember that education means more than expertise in just one limited area. Most curriculums require knowledge in both the sciences and liberal arts. Bear with the curriculum and eventually your courses will become more focused, especially in the upper level courses or in graduate school. You will find that all subjects are more interesting and easier to comprehend if you have some related knowledge to associate with the subject matter. Being older and experienced should give you a broader base of knowledge to complement new information.

How satisfying you find the successful completion of each assignment is important in maintaining a high degree of motivation. Share your successes with those interested in your educational efforts. Their support and praise can be uplifting and motivational. Don't hesitate to reward yourself with a walk in the park, a fishing trip, beach trip, etc.

Developing Your Listening Skills

Being a good listener requires concentration and practice. Just sitting in class while daydreaming about other issues in your life (and for the adult student there are plenty of other issues) will not get the grade you want. Listening to several hours of new material and concepts based on vocabulary that is unfamiliar is a misuse of your time. Listening to familiar terms related to concepts with which you have had some exposure, even though you may not completely understand them, can be a learning experience. Find a good pen or pencil, adjust your notes, sit up straight, and try to get into the instructor's thoughts in an effort to understand what he "means" and not simply what he "says." If you listen to the lecturer and reflect on his examples, the material will most likely begin to come together and you can ask pertinent questions once you know what parts are causing your confusion or uncertainty.

The bottom line is READ the assignment before trying to listen to the lecture. Be prepared. Stay ahead of the instructor. This way you have a knowledge base on which to build. You can associate what he is saying to your growing knowledge on the subject. You will be more relaxed and can take relevant notes which will be clearer to you later.

If you are simply unable to read the chapters before they are to be discussed in class, at least read the chapter summaries. Many undergraduate textbooks provide excellent chapter summaries and a review of key words. There is also an advantage to reviewing the notes from the last class before entering the classroom. Usually you can flip through class notes while grabbing a quick snack.

Taking Notes in Class

Taking notes that are useful later requires some technique and practice. You'll find the techniques below but you must provide the practice. As you listen to the lecture, select key points, organize them, and jot them down. Sometimes you may have to reorganize the material later. Your notes provide you with your own personal study guide. These notes are written in your style for only you to understand and to review. Good, complete notes make your learning more efficient. Keep your notes -- they are yours and you may need them later. It would surprise you how many professionals use their class notes later in their careers. As a matter of fact, your instructor may be using an updated version of his old class notes as the basis for his lectures.

Your note taking style should be flexible because different lecturers and different materials require different types of notes. Drawings, sketches, outlines, lists, or parts of sentences may each be appropriate at different times. It is a good practice to leave extra space in the margins for adding additional information to expand hurriedly written notes. You probably already use some abbreviations only you can decode. This is fine as long as you can easily decipher those symbols. However, to enhance your vocabulary, you should spell out new terms, especially in basic intro-type courses. As you continue in school, develop new symbols or short cuts for note taking.

Remember to listen and to only write down the important points. You can't record everything on paper. If you attempt to do this, you'll miss much of what is to be learned and understood from the lecture. You must select, organize, and then make notations. For this reason, it's best not to rely on actual shorthand for writing your notes. Again, you need to be listening, concentrating, selecting, organizing, and relating the information to your current base of knowledge for it to have meaning for you. For this same reason, using tape recordings of lectures may or may not increase your learning. When relying on tapes, you're more likely to ease up on your concentration because you say, "Oh, well, I can listen to this later."

It's a good practice to review your notes as soon after class as possible, maybe a coffee stop on your way home. Utilize the extra margin space to fill in information to complete your notes. For those notes that don't appear reasonable or clear because of missing details, make a special notation and talk to your instructor or a classmate about this information. We've all experienced the frustration of trying to understand "cold notes" taken weeks before. Review your notes from time to time -- don't wait until just before the exam. Following the exam, look back over your notes and evaluate how much help they were in preparing you. Use this evaluation to improve your note taking for the next course.

Using the Textbook

Most courses require you to purchase, one, two, or sometimes more books. It seems that the cost of texts have become a significant part of educational expenses. Many book stores, both on and off campus, will now buy used textbooks at the end of each quarter. They then resell these books at half the original cost. Not surprisingly, students generally keep the texts that are especially applicable to their major area of study, but it is interesting to note that students also tend to keep the books they used in courses they enjoyed.

With the investment you must make in textbooks, be sure to take every advantage of your books. If this means underlining and writing notes in the margins, do it. You want to transfer as much of the information in the book into your store of knowledge as possible. Good textbooks can be excellent reference materials in years to come. Ask instructors if they still refer to some of the books they studied while in school. The response will probably be affirmative, and they could probably list or show you several in their office.

Observe the format of the textbook. It should serve as an example for organizing your studying. Many have previews, subheadings, and certain words and phrases italicized or in bold print. Some have definitions of key words in the margin, diagrams providing a pictorial image, and a summary. Still others have sample questions at the end of each unit or chapter.

A good book should efficiently guide you through the material. If your book is in its second or later edition, it has probably proven its effectiveness and has been accepted by many colleges. It is probably thorough, well organized, and structured to serve as an excellent guide and companion to your classwork.

Regardless of how well organized and credible your book is, you will generally find the most recent citations and references are already two years old. This is especially true in fast changing areas of science. Your instructor may provide comments about recent studies he has learned of at conferences or from recent issues of professional journals. For this reason, in upper level courses, you may be assigned articles from journals to bring you up to date in specific areas. You should also become aware of opportunities for students to attend national, regional, or state conferences, and more recently, the tele-conference systems now available on your campus. All of these supplement your text and provide you more avenues for learning.

When studying a textbook, your objective is to obtain, store, relate, and be able to understand its contents for future use. Speed is not nearly as important as comprehension. Learning new material is an active, continuing process that can be greatly enhanced if you practice and perfect your study techniques. You want to relate new information to something said or presented earlier. Back and forth -- organizing, relating, and reorganizing are parts of the learning process.

Writing your own summaries, outlines, and questions from the text are useful learning techniques. A 3x5 card with notes and/or new vocabulary words with their meanings can be handy study guides to utilize while waiting in lines or sitting in traffic jams.

I've found that one of the most efficient ways to study and review textbook material is to underline major ideas in the text. By highlighting, you can review the entire chapter in a short time. But the secret to highlighting is to go back with a different color highlighter and underline only the key word or words on significant topics. When you review, look at these key terms. If there is any question in your mind about what was stated or if it's not clear, read a little more of the information on that topic. Probably the next time you review, the single word will suffice to freshen your memory. Using this technique, after several reviews of the chapter, you can sit down later and review the chapter in five minutes. Try it -- a little practice and you will be proficient at it.

Learning is different from memorizing. Memorized information will not be with you long if it's all piecemeal and fragmented. Nor is cramming at the last minute in the best interest of your grade nor your professional career as retention will be quite low. You've registered, paid tuition, invested in textbooks, and made a "B," but what have you gained? Unless you've truly learned the subject, you will eventually become confused and disappointed about what you gained from a course or from your college education. For information to be useful, it must be understood and remembered, it must be organized, grouped, attached, and made meaningful, which usually takes time and effort. Use these study tips to make the most of the time you have to devote to studying. You want to absorb and utilize the vast amount of information presented to you.

Preparing for and Taking Examinations

You've read the text, listened in class, taken good notes, and now exam day is rapidly approaching. It's true that how well you're doing the tasks just mentioned will be revealed by your grade, but the mechanics of actually taking exams require some basic techniques which come with experience. Different types of tests and questions require different types of preparation. While types of preparation may vary, the key to exams is "preparation."

First, find out when the exam will be given. This information should be on the class syllabus you received the first day. Pay attention to any date adjustments due to weather or illness. If you feel the same old anxiety that was a problem for you during earlier efforts at education, you'll find both chapters 7 and 8 helpful in overcoming this anxiety.

Scheduling your time is very important as you should discipline yourself to study at specific times. It's easy to say, "Well, I'll have time tomorrow or over the weekend," but tomorrow and the weekend may slip by before your intended study period begins -- especially if the weekend included a trip to the beach. Being away from your regular study setting makes it difficult to start or to concentrate on your studies.

Research has shown that most students accelerate their study efforts as the test date draws near. This procrastination results in cramming right up to the last minutes. Cramming is a poor way to learn or retain information for a period of time.

Preparing for the exam should be accomplished in many short study sessions rather than one or two marathon sessions. Retention is much better if you review the material a number of times. Your level of long-term retention may be of great benefit when you take the comprehensive final exam or tests in later courses.

The test provides you feedback for assessing your level of learning and for evaluating your study techniques. For this reason, it becomes a tool for further learning. Hopefully, your instructor will provide feedback, in the form of a graded exam, within a few days.

Learning is an active process and requires you to gradually gather a body of related knowledge. Listening, reading, reviewing, practicing, organizing, analyzing, and reviewing again are each a part of the process. Preparing some of your own practice tests works well for some, especially if you're studying with a partner or if you or your partner has taken exams from this instructor previously. Publishers sometimes provide helpful questions and study guides after each chapter or section in texts.

Become aware of the different types of exams. Traditional exams are given within the class period with no notes or other materials to assist you. Untraditional exams may include "open book" or "practical tests" given individually or to small groups. A word of caution -- open book tests are no snap. They can take you off stride if you aren't completely prepared. Often these exams are timed so you must be familiar with the material in your text. Practical tests may be appropriate in a lab course; for example, you may be asked to test a blood sample, identify and label anatomical parts of a specimen, etc. You may be graded on how you perform while solving the problem as well as your final answer. Again, good study techniques can help you prepare for these exams.

Another type of exam is the "take home" exam. Though you may have several days to complete this exam, it is wise to begin immediately. Organize your ideas and outline your responses. This can be one of the most difficult tests you'll ever take.

It is helpful to know what type of test questions you can expect on an exam. Some instructors prefer objective questions such as true or false, multiple choice, or matching, while others prefer essay questions. The size of the class, the type of material, and the instructor's preference are all involved in the decision. Objective tests are quite common in large classes with factual content. Some instructors have a mixture of questions -- something for everyone, so to speak. Below are a few helpful test taking hints:

True or False:

1. Try not to over-read a question. Read it carefully but don't read into it more than is written.

2. Absolute terminology, such as "always" or "never", is often false.

3. Qualifying terms, such as "sometimes" or "it appears", are usually true.

4. Generally longer statements are likely to be true.

5. Remember that if any part of the statement is false the entire statement is false.

6. Answer all questions even if you have to guess (unless there is a penalty for incorrect answers).

Multiple Choice Questions

1. Read the statement carefully and eliminate the two obviously incorrect choices.

2.   Usually your first choice or best guess is the one to stay with.

3.   Remember to pick the "best" choice as several may be partially correct.

4.   Be sure to read all choices before answering.

5.   If you're not sure of one answer, continue with the next question. Later questions may provide a clue to the correct answer for a particularly difficult question.

6.   Be sure to check that all questions are answered.

There are other types of questions that require you to fill in blanks or to write short essays. These are the most difficult for many students. Requiring total recall of correct information, these questions may instruct you to discuss, explain, or compare. To do this requires a thorough understanding of the material. Be extra careful that you understand what the question is asking you to do. Does it say describe, discuss, compare, or criticize?

How you organize and present your answers are important since the one doing the grading must assess your knowledge from your written response. Attempt to be straight-forward and factual rather than wordy and repetitious.

Again, use the results from your tests to evaluate your study techniques. Are they working for you in this class? What changes would improve your performance?

One last comment on your study technique. A study partner or a small study group can be helpful. If you over hear some students arranging a study session, introduce yourself and ask to join. You will probably be eagerly accepted. Or you can easily organize your own group by asking one or two other students in class. However, this can easily be a waste of your time if the others in the group are not serious about learning. Discussions must be focused or else they often stray to other topics, classes, or instructors. A good focused group with members who arrive prepared and serious can be an asset to your study efforts.

Using the Library

It never ceases to amaze me how some students get a college degree without learning to use the library. For the more serious student, the library can be like a candy store, so much to try but so little money, or so much information but so little time.

The library is where your education can really rocket to great heights. Most of your classes will only introduce you to ideas, familiarize you with terminology, and provide general theories and major proponents of particular areas. The library stands as the major source of knowledge as we know it today.

If you're near a large city, you may have access to a complete municipal library, but normally your college library will provide you with the specific information you need for your courses. The instructors are familiar with the library on campus and therefore coordinate their assignments with what's available there.

A problem for many students is how to get the information from the library shelves and/or computers into a form they can assimilate and utilize. Once you've learned the basic organization of your library, you'll be pleased to find most library systems are quite similar. The ability to use the library effectively and efficiently can be an asset for you and your career for years to come.

As a returning student, you are interested and serious about learning and you need to do it efficiently. Therefore, you should go to the library the first week of your course and begin seeking, searching, exploring, and questioning. Browse, locate information, try the microfilm machines, call up indexes on the computer, and ask a few questions.

Most campus libraries offer one or two orientation courses for credit which are open to all students. Even if you attended one of these in the past, as a returning student you'll be surprised at the many changes in library systems as a result of computers which are great tools if you take time to learn to use them. Your library may offer a two or four hour workshop to familiarize its patrons with new systems and services.

Do not hesitate to ask questions. Library professionals are proud of their chosen careers. Most are eager to share their knowledge about the library system with students. For example, if the book you want is not on the shelves, ask about its location. The staff can check to see if the book is checked out, when it should be returned, if it's been put on reserve, or perhaps temporarily taken out of circulation for binding.

Probably the basic component of any library is the card catalog, a file listing every book in the library. These cards are usually in the lobby within sight of the circulation desk. Books are listed on these cards alphabetically in three categories: subject, title, and author. If you're not familiar with a new subject, you should start with the subject listing, write down those listings that appear from the card description to be what you're seeking, and use the number code to locate the books. When you find your specific book, you'll probably find other interesting books related to your topic in the same area.

Other useful components of the library include the circulation desk, reference desk, government documents desk, and perhaps a reserve desk. Their names literally convey their functions: the circulation desk handles the check-out and return of those books which can be taken from the library; the reference desk directs you to reference material in abstracts and periodicals; the government documents desk explains and guides you to the array of government reports; and the reserve desk shelves material which can be used only a limited time, maybe a few hours or overnight. An instructor may put special material which he wants all the class to read on reserve so it is equally available to everyone. In such a case, you may find another copy in the library or you may be able to obtain a copy through the interlibrary loan system. By completing a simple request form, the interlibrary system allows you to retrieve material held by other libraries in the system. Normally the system will search the files and bring you the information or specific book from the nearest source within a few days.

The most recent information on a specific subject will be found in periodicals or professional journals. Just as the medical profession has its credible journals, so do other professions including psychology, sociology, biology, criminal justice, etc. Learning to retrieve information from these journals should be one of your early objectives. Each specific area has its own abstracts and indexes. Currently this information can be brought up on computers and printed for your convenience. For example, PsyLit provides current abstracts for many of the social sciences. Examples of other useful sources include the ERIC System, Dialog, Academic Index and the Reader's Guide to Periodical Literature.

Learn to use microfilms. Many libraries have special sections to house these films. Because they are cheaper, libraries can provide you more information on a limited budget.

If your university has a medical, veterinary, or law school, these schools probably have separate libraries on campus. Their books and journals are generally indexed in the main library system. Their card catalog entries indicate that they are found in the special library.

Another note of interest is especially true for the larger departments within the university system.   There may be a collection of books and materials pooled by faculty or purchased from departmental budgets. These materials are very specific to a particular department and are not accessible through the main library.

Again, familiarize yourself with the library as soon as possible. This is where you'll develop the professional expertise that determines your success in your chosen area.

Preparing Special Assignments

In addition to exams, you may be required to write a term paper, to make an oral presentation, or to complete a research project. The basic procedures for preparing these assignments are essentially the same: understand the assignment; start early; locate materials; write an outline and let it sit a few days; re-write; write the first draft; add references and footnotes; prepare a final draft; proofread the finished product and/or organize the details for the presentation.

First, ask questions if you're not clear on what's required. What is the expected length? How many references are required: How should references be cited? When is the project due? What are format requirements such as margins, running heads, and title page?

Start your assignment early. If you have a choice of topics, select one that interests you, not too broad nor too focused. Most of your information will probably come from the library. Secure the information as early as possible so you will have plenty of time to utilize the interlibrary loan program if necessary.

Organize your materials as they accumulate and start an outline for the paper. At this time, you should be aware of what else you will need, how the paper is to be organized, where it's going, and how it will get there. Set it aside a few days but jot down ideas or changes that pop into your mind which you may want to include. Some useful ideas may emerge during this incubation period and others may be discarded. Make sure you maintain complete reference information. There are different suggestions for listing references but usually you will be expected to provide the author's name, date of publication, title of book or article, name and volume of journal, and page numbers. If the source is a book, the name and location of the publisher is required. Some formats require page numbers for direct quotations. As you make notes and begin your drafts, make certain that you record the details you need for references.

Because your first draft is a working copy, double space and leave wide margins. Erase, mark over, and make whatever changes are necessary. If you're comfortable on a word processor, it will make the adjustments easier. Once you're satisfied with the working draft, prepare the final copy for proofing and submission. As was emphasized before, make sure you understand how your instructor wants the footnotes and references cited.

Before giving your paper to the instructor, proofread again and correct punctuation and spelling. Be sure you satisfy both content and format requirements. While your content may be excellent, you won't receive the grade you want if you fail to follow instructions. There are widely accepted standardized formats for research reports: a title, brief but complete; an introduction specifying the reason for this study; a review of literature and a hypothesis; a method that explains what was done, to whom, by what means, and how; the results showing data in tables or graphs along with statistical results; and a discussion which interprets the results and draws conclusion. Many instructors will direct you to follow the basic requirements of the <u>American Psychological Association Manual</u> or the <u>MLA Handbook for Writers of Research Papers.</u> Most bookstores and libraries have copies of these manuals.

If the project is to be presented orally, you can use your completed paper by highlighting a xerox copy to emphasize the main point. You may want to use a separate outline or index cards for the oral presentation. Practice actually making the presentation, check the time and your pronunciation. If speaking before a group has created excessive anxiety for you in the past, read Chapter 7. Practice until you are comfortable with your content and delivery. Confidence gained through practice can help alleviate your anxiety. Again, practice, organize, and practice again for a good presentation.

Research projects are valuable learning tools which allow you to gain more knowledge on particular topics than your instructor or text presents. Regardless of the project, whether oral or written, the time spent in preparing it is usually reflected in the grade. Therefore, an early start and continuous reorganization

are important in producing the quality project you anticipate --
the quality required to earn the grade you want.

Summary

I hope you have found this chapter informative and that it
will aid in your pursuit of the education you're seeking. While
most of us are aware of our weakest areas, we need to evaluate
our efforts fairly and objectively. By utilizing the hints for learning
in this chapter, you can evaluate both your strengths and
weaknesses in your effort to attain the most from your educational
endeavors.

PART II

On and Off Campus Impediments and Distractions

This section describes and addresses personal issues faced by many older students. Usually there is a catalyst that triggers the return to school. This may be something good, perhaps more free time, the children having grown up, retirement, or financial security. More often, however, the catalyst is a crisis or disruption in life, perhaps the loss of a job, divorce or death of a spouse, abuse, or depression. All of these events can contribute to low self-esteem and a search for new meaning in life.

Chapters 4 and 5 are written by a counselor and a psychologist respectively. These authors focus on issues that frequently promulgate a woman's return to school. For example, in Chapter 4, Susan Dudley prepares the student for feelings of guilt, discusses how to handle the frustrations of functioning in multiple roles, and offers advice on satisfying conflicting demands. In Chapter 5, Carolyn Thomas shares her expertise in the area of family abuse which, more often than we care to admit, is an incentive to renewing efforts for higher education. Releasing inhibitions and utilizing new freedoms provide a new focus on career and education visions.

Recognition of specific problems, awareness that these problems are experienced by many, and evidence that others have successfully faced and overcome these obstacles all tend to relieve and energize potential students. The success story introducing this part emphasizes that confidence, determination, and courage have, for others, led to the achievement of long-held goals and ambitions.

JANE'S STORY

After being out of high school for ten years, the decision to begin college again was most difficult. I was in a personal turmoil: a failing marriage, no job, and two small children who needed me at home. I received virtually no encouragement from my husband which delayed my decision considerably. On the other hand, I was fortunate as my parents, other family members and friends were always there to provide the support I needed. After being confused and guilt-ridden for some time, I forced myself to slow down, relax and consider my options.

Basically, I had two options. Option number one was the safer -- continue with the "status quo." I could do what I had done for ten years and was expected to do, stay at home, depend on my husband, raise my children in the "proper manner," keep the house in perfect order, and be the support system for anyone needing a shoulder. I knew that this was not me and I offer no apology for it. A person must be theirself first. So much for option number one!

Option number two was somewhat more courageous. I could combine my first option with attending college. I knew it could be done; in fact, some friends had successfully tried it. This was what I really wanted to do even though I realized how difficult it would be. Once I made this decision, I began making plans.

First I had to find a place for my children to stay. Since they had never been away from me, I wanted to find just the right childcare. Though I found that special place and it honestly worked out well, I still had doubts and concerns about leaving my children. No one had prepared me for the guilt feelings as I left two long faces at the door; I knew both children cried as I drove away.

After the children and I adjusted to the separation, it was time to take the plunge -- registration. I had forgotten what administrative red tape was all about but I was quickly reminded. With a little advice from my justice and public safety counselor, I survived registration. I had attended the same college for a few quarters immediately after high school graduation; I was thrilled to find my former counselor still with the same department. He even remembered me and provided much appreciated support and advice.

On the first day of classes, I was accompanied by a little anxiety and great expectations. Walking around the campus after being away for so long, I saw only very young faces; I couldn't help but wonder what these young students saw in my face! They could have been thinking that I looked out of place, too old for college, or perhaps they simply thought I was just stupid for not having finished college when I was "supposed" to. Later I discovered this was not the case at all; in fact, some even admired us "oldies" for coming back. Actually some younger students have come to me for guidance and advice; this is an unexpected reward and pleasure.

I was relieved as well as a little surprised at the number of older people in college. I had several in my classes and soon realized I was not alone nor was I a freak. Each "oldie" had a different story but the objectives or goals were quite similar. Sharing experiences and reasons for being in school gave us a sense of belonging.

I recall one man's story very well as it touched me to the point of becoming an inspiration that I still fall back on during tough times. This man had worked for the same company for more than 20 years and was considered one of its foremost engineers. His wife had recently died, and he also had a heart condition. Six months before his scheduled retirement, he lost his job because of a company sell-out. He was crushed and confused. Because he felt he couldn't work for another company in a similar capacity, he felt compelled to change his career at age 59! He enrolled as a business major and did very well while enjoying the frequent opportunities to share his "real life" experiences with younger students. His courage to change and begin a second career should give us all hope.

My classes were more interesting than I had remembered or perhaps time had improved my ability to concentrate as well as my level of interest. For whatever reason, I now look forward to attending class rather than behaving as I had at 18 -- looking for excuses to cut or even sleeping through class. Many younger students appear to take their educational opportunities for granted; maybe I did at that age. I know now how much education means and that it is a privilege. I realize the difference an education can make in my life and in the future of my children.

Not only have the names and faces changed at college but so have my perspectives and attitudes toward the many different aspects of learning. One major change is my positive attitude about studying. Even though it may seem impossible to get the motivation and the concentration together when I do find the time to study, it certainly pays off. As a young student, my study habits had not been up to par and my grades reflected both this and my lack of interest.

One new study skill is reserving a certain time of day as my study time. This time changes each quarter so that it always fits in with my class schedule and other responsibilities. I view my study time as an important appointment which cannot be broken. If something or someone infringes on this time -- unless it is a true emergency -- I simply say, "I'm sorry but I can't; I have an appointment." Even my young children understand they must entertain themselves during this time. Another helpful hint for a lecture class is a tape recorder. I listen to recorded lectures in my car, as I cook, etc. These recordings are particularly helpful when preparing for tests. In classes requiring heavy reading, I outline each chapter, highlighting the important sections. If I maintain a consistent pattern using these techniques, I find that everything else falls into place and I generally meet all deadlines. This alone relieves any stress or guilt I might have suffered because of time demands.

At the end of my first quarter, I was surprised at my reflections on being an older student. I was pleased with how much I had learned in each class. At 18 I had received final grades and wondered why I had not gained any knowledge or understanding of the subject. Today I seek understanding of the subject through concentration in class and redefined study habits. I want to comprehend and retain information; I am eager to learn! Because I now stay on top of what is expected of me, college is more fun plus I feel better about myself. My education has given me a sense of personal satisfaction. This feeling is most important to those of us who have felt guilty about spending our valuable time at school instead of with our families.

Though minor to some, my accomplishments have had a major impact on my life. Professionally, I am closer to attaining a B.S. degree in criminal justice, a science that I believe in. After graduation I plan to work with juvenile delinquents in some capacity. I have been encouraged in this area and feel there is a great need for people who care what happens to today's youth.

At the time I returned to college, my marriage was failing and has since ended in divorce. Of course my return to college affected our problems, but in all sincerity, I don't believe my marriage would have lasted even if I had settled for my former status quo. My ex-husband felt jealous or threatened by my new sense of independence and what he perceived as my leaving the protected life he offered.

On a more positive note, my children have adjusted beautifully to the changes in their lives due to divorce and college. My six year old believes she should make only A's and B's because Mommy does. I'm pleased that my efforts encourage her to do her best. Because I value the time I have with my children, I try to make each moment count! I also see my education as a helpful tool in my personal goal of raising two well adjusted, independent children.

Personally, returning to college has bolstered my self-confidence as well as my strength and determination. Professionally, new doors are opening for me; I am eager for my future career. Realistically and honestly, starting over is complicated and mind-boggling, but for me it has proven a very satisfying, fulfilling experience.

Chapter 4

DEALING WITH CONFLICTING DEMANDS

Susan Dudley

Returning students often must balance new commitments to education against continuing commitments to family and home. Conflicts between the roles of wife or mother and the role of student can cause guilt, anxiety, and depression. These conflicts ultimately lead some returning students to abandon attempts at education. This chapter deals with the issue of role conflict and offers practical advice on how you, as a returning student, can learn to cope with conflicting demands and recognize the value of pursuing personal goals in spite of some necessary family adjustments.

When you make the decision to return to school to get the education that you want for a more challenging or better-paying job, you expect substantial relief from the frustrations that have guided (or driven) you back to academia. But instead, many returning students feel just the opposite of relief. They experience guilt, feelings of imminent failure, and a sure sense that they will not be able to meet the responsibilities of being a wife, mother, homemaker, and student. After spending some years as a homemaker, or working wife, you might already feel some guilt for having abandoned education earlier in your life. Perhaps you worry that if you hadn't "quit" before, you wouldn't be in an unsatisfactory position today. Your discontent is motivating you to go back and do what "normal" people did when they were still young and free of the responsibilities of marriage, children, and home.

In addition to guilt for life decisions, you may also worry about the wisdom of following the path you are presently undertaking. As a returning student, you may fear that your pursuit of a university degree is selfish, is benefiting no one, and is robbing other family members of the time and attention they deserve from you. When the demands are especially difficult to meet, some returning students reason that giving up school will eliminate their guilt. They also have doubts about returning to the circumstances that originally convinced them that they needed something more challenging. (And they will have "quit" once again!)

Although taking on the new role of student, you will continue to function in more familiar roles as wife, mother, and homemaker. Do not confuse compromise, digression, or interruption in your progress with "quitting." We've all been taught that "quitters never win, and winners never quit." While the wisdom of this philosophy may apply in athletic competitions, experience shows that it is not necessarily a reasonable approach to life in general. Sometimes you have to "quit," if quitting means that you must deviate from the straight-line path to a goal. It is important to learn that temporary delays are not failures.

During my own college and graduate school years, I was caught in an unrelenting love-hate relationship with academia. I went through school in starts and stops. The interruptions or periods when I had decided to give up altogether on education were never satisfactory. Neither were the periods when I was actively enrolled in degree programs. My experience is far from unique. What causes this kind of ambivalence in the older student?

Part of the explanation lies in the fear of leaving old and accepted female roles in order to strike out in pursuit of new challenges at school. For me, decisions to leave school were usually driven by feelings of guilt. On top of the guilt, pursuing my degree was hard work. This hard work offered little short term satisfaction. It certainly deprived my husband of the traditional helpmate he had presumably bargained for when we married. I always had a strong sense that I <u>should</u> go back to the familiar roles of traditional wife and homemaker, that I should leave my ambitions and fantasies behind. After all, school was for youngsters.

Why does guilt play such an overwhelming role in some of our most important decisions? This guilt can be attributed, at least in part, to the dilemma at the heart of many women's lives: women have been taught that their proper role is to enjoy the "selfless" pleasures of giving and loving. On the other hand, the pleasures derived from finding your own place in the world outside your home and family are regarded as "selfish" pleasures when women (but not men) are concerned. Whether selfless or selfish, women suffer overwhelming guilt over the decision to return to school.

The colloquial image of being "caught between a rock and a hard place" comes to mind. Some returning women students find there is no way to gain control of their lives without sacrifice. Long-held ideals about proper and acceptable female behavior might need to be modified, but the long-term rewards of accepting the risk are great.

Most women have been taught to worry about the opinions other people have of them. They fear being criticized for going to school and "abandoning" traditional roles and responsibilities. On the other hand, now there is fear of being criticized for giving up or quitting after having made the commitment to return to school. The "superwoman" solution to this dilemma ultimately traps many women in an exhausting cycle with few real rewards. Superwomen are determined to prove to the world that they <u>can</u> have it all. According to the superwoman ideal, neither husband, children, nor friends will be inconvenienced by their adding another full-time responsibility to their lives!

Sociologists and psychologists have described the "housewife syndrome" and the "working wife syndrome" as manifestations of this dilemma. Although many returning students are divorced or separated, most analyses of women's problems are built from the perspective of how a <u>wife</u> might fit in other pursuits rather that how a woman might fit marriage into an otherwise fulfilling life. You may recognize yourself in these descriptions, regardless of your marital status. Each of these syndromes describes a role in which fulfillment and happiness are blocked. Self-esteem suffers because of the demands of either situation. Feeling the pressure of both, the returning student is often caught between the two syndromes. Together they can create a trap for which students are especially vulnerable.

The Housewife Syndrome

The role of the housewife has been greatly romanticized. Television images of the ever cheerful 1950s vintage homemaker, baking cookies, wearing high heeled shoes and a starched apron, abound. But comparisons of real housewives and working wives demonstrate that housewives have lower self-esteem, a greater sense of powerlessness, and lower participation in family decision-making. In addition, housewives who are not employed outside the home complain of more physical problems, such as headaches and fatigue, as well as more psychological symptoms, such as depression and guilt.

Among the factors contributing to the apparent discontent and malaise of housewives is the fact that they often do not get appropriate recognition for their work. They have no clear criteria for success, and they get no paycheck to boost their self-esteem. To illustrate these points, consider the results of a survey done by Myra Marx Ferree in 1976. Ferree questioned 135 working class women, some of whom were housewives and some of whom were employed in pink-collar jobs such as waiting tables, sales, or hairdressing. Only 7% of the housewives reported that they were "extremely good" at taking care of their homes, and 75% felt incompetent. In contrast, while 66% of the working wives said that they were poor homemakers, <u>none</u> said they were incompetent at their jobs. In fact, 50% said they were "extremely good" at their jobs!

In another study by Phillip Shaver and Jonathan Freedman, 46% of housewives reported that they felt anxious and worried. Only 28% of employed wives shared these feelings. Similar differences were obtained when the women were asked whether they felt lonely or worthless.

Data of this sort may not surprise you. As a returning female student, you may recognize yourself in descriptions of the housewife syndrome. You know first hand that such feelings, dissatisfactions, and discontent have contributed directly or indirectly to your decision to return to school. You are trying to redirect your energies into channels other than homemaking. By knowing what brought you back to school, you probably find yourself even more distressed when you contemplate why being in school is so stressful. The comparisons cited above would seem to indicate that going to school would offer to the homemakers the kind of satisfactions that the working wife group expressed. The returning student should be feeling better, and not worse. And that brings us to the working wife syndrome.

The Working Wife Syndrome

Arlie Hochschild's recent surveys on housework show that housewives work 53 hours per week. Perhaps surprisingly, this figure has not changed in 40 years, in spite of new household technologies and higher family income levels bringing automatic washing machines and dishwashers, for example, into more private homes. In contrast to the full-time homemaker, working wives spend 26 hours per week on housework. This is in addition to the 40 hours they devote to their full-time jobs. The working wife gets no more outside help, and no more help from her husband than does the full-time homemaker. In fact, data indicate that husbands of employed women spend an average of 36 minutes per week on household maintenance!

If employed wives have substantially fewer hours of free time per week than either housewives or employed men, it is no surprise that the working wife syndrome includes feelings of depression and incompetence as well as psychosomatic ailments such as insomnia and stomach aches. In practical terms, a working wife has two jobs, while a working husband has only one!

Our culture expects women to handle the conflicting demands from job and family. Studies have shown that women experience greater conflict between their outside work and their marriages and families than men do. For example, when a child is ill, the working mother is much more likely to stay home from work. Similarly, when extra time at the workplace would yield either personal or material reward, a woman is more likely than a man to forego such rewards if family obligations conflict.

Modern language usage reflects society's expectations. For example, linguistically and perhaps also from the perspective of division of labor, you would not be surprised to hear a woman say happily that her husband "helps" around the house. Or a man might say he has been "babysitting" the kids in his wife's absence. Both statements clearly imply that the responsibility for housework and childcare is the wife's. The husband is free to relieve the wife of her responsibilities at his pleasure. On the other hand, you would probably be astonished to hear a woman say that she often "helps" around the house or "babysits" her children!

Relating these Syndromes to the Returning Student

Bringing this back to the realm of the returning student, you can see that the female student, who is juggling the demands of her home against demands of school, is in a position that is not very different from that of the working wife. This is particularly true if academic performance is taken seriously, as most returning students of both sexes do. If you are like many other returning students, you probably feel a need to devote substantial amounts of time to your studies. This will be exaggerated if you lack confidence in your ability to study and learn effectively, so that going back to school often equates to a commitment to a full-time job. Unfortunately, as a student, you don't have the benefit of a paycheck at the end of the week. Your student experience includes most of the same sacrifices that the working wife endures, but your family does not enjoy the tangible benefit of extra income in return for your new preoccupation and non-availability.

Role Strain

The result of the housewife syndrome and the working wife syndrome and the conflicts they produce is described by a concept that sociologists call role strain. Role strain occurs when we try to meet the responsibilities of two, sometimes mutually exclusive, roles. Satisfaction of one set of requirements will necessarily mean that the second set of requirements will not be met. The result of role strain, predictably, is the kind of guilt and sense of failure that so often plague the returning student's life.

In general, working student-husbands do not suffer the kind of role strain that student-wives experience. In our culture, the role of married man and the role of working man are not in conflict and do not require mutually exclusive activities. The old idea that a "great woman" stands behind every "great man" is derived from the fact that the support functions performed by the traditional wife freed her husband for other concerns. No one thinks to ask whether the successful male employee will be able to maintain his job performance after his children are born! He can work late into the evening, confident that his wife will see to dinner for their children. He need not worry whether there will be clean clothes, supplies in the cupboard, or social obligations met. He can depend on his wife to deal with these things. A working husband can devote himself in a far more single-minded fashion to his work when he is provided these services by his wife.

As a student-wife, you probably have no one to provide this support for you. Instead, you likely will continue to provide most of these services for your family while you are going to school. The role strain then, especially for you as a returning student who is desperately trying to avoid "inconveniencing" your family, can cause substantial distress. The result is that you can be left emotionally drained, overwhelmed, and resentful of school demands. You may become resentful of the high standards that you've set for your performance and feel guilty for returning to school.

Role strain is highly characteristic of women who are trying to combine high prestige careers (or high grade point averages) with family obligations. It must be emphasized that the pressure on a woman to do well at school is usually great. After all, you fear you are sacrificing the well-being of your family, selfishly devoting time to yourself instead of exclusively to them. If you were to compromise on the quality of your school performance, you would be even more strongly tempted to declare your ambition "folly." Women students identify with and immediately embrace the truth of the adage that "women have to be twice as good to be taken half as seriously."

Solutions

The role of the successful student (or the high prestige professional) requires some degree of selfishness. This requirement should not be seen as a personality trait, but as a role requirement. Much as you may try to schedule your academic pursuits during the hours that your children are in school, and to confine your studying to time when your husband is otherwise occupied, there are always unforseen emergencies (or unexpected opportunities) that will require you to "rob" family members of your attention in order to attend to school responsibilities. For example, you have a paper due at 8 a.m. tomorrow, a lab project that requires a few more hours than expected, or an interesting speaker is scheduled to be on campus this evening. As a student you will learn that sometimes you must "selfishly" seize the time if you are to succeed in your academic pursuits. If you worry about cooking meals for the family, dusting the bookshelves, or "being there" to cheer your spouse after he's had a hard day, you may not finish your own work. If you try to "do it all" you will feel the strain in terms of exhaustion and resentment, and ultimately you may seek escape along the route of least resistance: giving up on school. "After all," some students say to themselves, "I made it this far without that degree, I don't really need it, and I can't juggle all of this and ask my family to sacrifice for my selfish dreams." You may be acutely aware that the price you will pay for being selfish about what you feel you need to do will be immeasurable guilt. The solution is to recognize that much of this guilt is self-generated, and to learn to give up the guilt traps that you build for yourself!

Self-Esteem

It is immeasurably important that you take the time required to do your work without suffering over your own perceived selfishness. You must learn to value your needs as highly as you value the needs of other people around you. The recognition that what you are doing is worthwhile and deserves some accommodation from your family members grows out of basic self-esteem. When you learn to see yourself as important, you also learn to evaluate your own needs realistically. You learn to give up the feeling that you don't deserve the consideration that you are asking from your husband and children.

Unfortunately in our society, strong self-esteem is sometimes incompatible with our expectations of the "good wife" or "good mother" who puts the well-being of her family ahead of herself in all things. There are many good books available to help you build your self-esteem. Learning to take other people's compliments seriously and to take honest pride in your own accomplishments are good signs that you are able to see yourself in the same positive light that others see you. This can relieve role strain substantially.

Your role strain can also be lightened if your family is openly supportive and if you can give them the freedom to be unselfish when that's what will help Mom get through her day. If your family is not openly supportive or if they are openly hostile, gaining self-esteem may be a slower process. Let us continue with other solutions to role strain that you can pursue.

Reassessment of Needs and Goals

Returning to school and taking on the new responsibilities that are part of that commitment implies that you have already been through some degree of personal reassessment. An aspect of this process, however, which sometimes isn't recognized and therefore isn't dealt with, is reassessment of your own goals. This reassessment should be relative to the role you have formerly maintained in the family and in the larger society. As we have seen, simply adding new responsibilities to an already full day can lead to frustration, exhaustion, and guilt. The reassessment that includes sorting through your old expectations for yourself, which have been rendered outmoded by the acceptance of your new goals and responsibilities, can yield new freedom....the freedom and right to incorporate your student status into your life without some of the role strain that would otherwise be there.

For example, in your role as homemaker, you may have taken pride in moving the refrigerator periodically to clean the floor underneath it. In your newer role as returning student, you may find that the goal of spotless floors becomes less important. Give yourself permission to abandon old, unsuitable goals when they no longer reflect current aspirations!

Sometimes honest self-assessment will allow you to relinquish your claim to the goal of providing total care for your family, enabling you to recognize that they are able to do things for themselves that you formerly did for them. What's more, they are probably able to do things for you in the spirit of mutual support that people who love each other will ideally maintain.

You may discover, under honest examination, that some of your former goals never were "yours" but were incorporated into your life as part of what you believed others expected of you. Do I clean my oven because I want my oven cleaned, or because I have learned that my mother values a clean oven? What will my mother say if she hears that I haven't cleaned my oven with the same regularity that she expects of herself? Can I live with that? I can give myself permission to let my mother set her own goals, while I set mine! It is hard to overstate the freedom that comes from discovering which of our homemaking goals are real for us, and which are superficial and can be abandoned.

Again, an important part of taking this step is giving yourself permission to change your direction. As your self-esteem grows, you will learn to accept more and more aspects of yourself as valuable, and you can learn to realistically live with the idea that, though there may be dust on the bookshelves, you are earning the grades you want.   When you learn to derive satisfaction from striving for your new goals, you can let go of the guilt of having abandoned an old goal that you no longer value as you did before.

Assertiveness

Learning to recognize what you really want and to believe that you deserve to have your needs met are the first steps toward learning to relieve role strain and guilt, the next step is learning to express your needs to your family and friends in clear and honest ways. This is the key to "assertive" behavior, which has little to do with getting your own way, but everything to do with honest communication. Through assertive action, your needs can be accommodated without manipulation, without aggression, without resentment, and without guilt.

Again, the traditional female role often does not give women the freedom to ask for what they want in direct ways.   Many women grow up learning to "suffer in silence" when other people fail to read their minds accurately!   On the other hand, some women learn to get what they want by being manipulative. These women are sometimes characterized as users of "feminine wiles." Sometimes they are recognized as intolerable martyrs. Still others learn to resort to unnecessary aggression, sarcasm, or put-downs of other people to get what they want.   Any of these modes is bound to lead to dissatisfaction, if not in the short-term, certainly in the long term.

When you learn to assert your needs and desires honestly, you also learn to deal with other people honestly, so that mutual respect is fostered and everyone around you has an opportunity to live in an environment free of hidden emotional traps. This is not to say that assertive behavior is always welcomed without resistance from people who may be used to dealing with you in less honest ways. But assertive behavior will at least enable you to feel clear about what your goals are and allow others the opportunity to accommodate you, without having to guess what you want from them. Books and classes are available to help you learn to use assertive behaviors in constructive ways that will help ease role strain. You will find more about assertiveness in Chapter 7.

Successful Role Combinations

Adjustments that will allow you as a returning student to make successful role combinations will ultimately protect your psychological and physical health. In addition to taking steps to improve your self-esteem, clarify your goals, and communicate assertively with your loved ones. These adjustments often involve tension and stress-management techniques.

Cognitive restructuring. For example, when evaluating your life situations, it is more useful to look at and talk about (even in internal dialogues with yourself) the <u>benefits</u>, rather than the costs of combining school (and later, career) and family. This is a technique psychologists call cognitive restructuring. It could take the form of the following sorts of statements: "I am a better mother, for providing my children with a role model of a woman who pursues goals and deals successfully with extra-family demands" or "My children benefit from the fact that my energies are not expended on 'over-mothering.'"

Compartmentalization of roles. A second successful technique employs compartmentalization of the two roles to keep them as distinct as possible. Many women are adept at this already, judging from the fact that fewer women than men bring work home with them. Of course, there is an inherent trap here. If you compartmentalize because of fear that your family will not accept your alternate role, you will likely be adding to your guilt and role strain. On the other hand, if you compartmentalize positively, because you have realized that both your roles are legitimate and worthy of your dedication, then you are, in effect, giving yourself permission to make the most of your time at school, just as you have made the most of your family commitments.

Advance planning. Conflict between roles is inevitable, and you should not ignore the fact that there will be times when special circumstances will force you to give precedence to one role over the other. Advance consideration and planning can help to prevent these situations from taking you completely by surprise and overwhelming you with a sense of failure and/or guilt. For example, it is common for women to give family crises precedence over work or school obligations. Such decisions need not lead to guilt feelings if they are worked out in advance. Conversely, you will probably want the freedom to expect family forbearance when class demands are especially high, such as during exams, or when papers are being prepared.

Compromise. This suggests another important stress management tool, compromise. It is very common for wives to control the extent of their school and career commitments to fit their family circumstances. For example, considerations regarding how your husband's work is going, his income, the ages of your children, your husband's support (or lack of it), and your own academic goals will probably guide your decisions about how you will integrate your work and family roles. Wives usually expect little from their families in terms of help in adjusting to their career demands, and any sign of accommodation on the part of family members often leaves women feeling guilty.

It is critical here to recognize that your own goals and aspirations are as valid as those of any of the other family members. As discussed above, self-esteem exercises may help promote such recognition. It is also valuable to recognize that your children learn from watching your behavior, as well as from the opportunities you allow them. It is valuable then, to teach your children to compromise with you and to make concessions in their expectations of you, so your outside goals can be reached and their independence is fostered. Perhaps as important as any other aspect of allowing your children to learn to accommodate your needs, just as you do your best to accommodate theirs, is that this will ultimately strengthen their abilities to live constructively and happily with other people. For many women, this goes against years of training through which they have learned that the appropriate role for women in families is to be the provider of love and support rather than the recipient. The world will undoubtedly be a better place when both women and men are able to embrace <u>both</u> of those roles with equal ease!

Working on your own terms. As your self-esteem and power to set your own goals increase, you will begin to feel more comfortable working on your own terms, rather than adopting work behavior that you think other people expect of you. This may include studying certain subjects and skimming others that hold no intrinsic interest for you. It may mean taking time off in the summer, to spend extra time with your children or cleaning the floor under the refrigerator. Working on your own terms may mean temporarily putting some projects on hold and giving priority to others. For example, you may decide to set aside your volunteer work for the PTA for the time being or you may decide that the PTA is too important for you to drop, and that maintaining a "B" grade point average instead of "A's" will allow you to honor and enjoy some of your other commitments while going to school.

Don't be afraid to make compromises with yourself. Sometimes you will find that your biggest conflicts stem from mutually exclusive expectations you honestly hold for yourself. Deciding to compromise on these expectations is legitimate and helpful. Recognize that you can only do so much, and that temporary shifts in your priorities, and that letting some things slide while you attend to others do not necessarily reflect any long-term change in your character or worth.

Similarly, don't be afraid to digress off the straightest path to your goal, if that straight path is not making you happy, or is interfering more than you can accept with your other responsibilities. Delays do not equate to failure, and working toward your goals in sane ways and at a sane pace will ultimately make your school experience more rewarding.

Working with others. A critical point to remember here is that the essence of successful role management is that it is always done in conjunction with others. Friends and relatives have to be amenable to the new rules governing your life. You will also find that, within limits, your professors will be sympathetic to the fact that the demands on your time are different from those of the more conventional student, and sometimes accommodations can be made on that end as well. Be prudent, however, in asking for special consideration on deadlines, etc. Your professors will lose patience if they think their goodwill is being taken advantage of.

Support groups. Successful women, women who have made acceptable role combinations, seem to have one crucial element in common, and that is the goodwill and support of other people in their lives. Part of this support, as you have seen, hinges on learning to accept what others offer. Organizations for returning students, or other support groups are often very helpful in keeping us mindful that we are not alone and that our problems are common to others who live in similar circumstances. We should remain aware that our conflicts regarding family and school are generated by social circumstances as well as individual circumstances.

Gaining perspective. Working through role combinations is an ongoing process. Role strain won't necessarily leave your life when you graduate and move on to other extra-familial pursuits, but you will probably find that school has provided you with the proverbial "trial by fire." It won't last forever, but it may be the hardest role strain you will have to face!

Learn during these years not to see your own compromises as failures. Individual women fighting a centuries-old culture have to move at a pace their own circumstances allow. Keep your ultimate goals in mind, and realize that the straight line path is not necessarily the only way to get there.

References

Ferree, M. M. (1976).   The Confused American Housewife. <u>Psychology Today</u>, 10, p. 76-80.

Hochschild, A. R. (1989). <u>The Second Shift: Working Parents and the Revolution.</u> New York: Viking.

Shaver, P., and Freedman, J. (1976). Your Pursuit of Happiness. <u>Psychology Today</u>, 10, p. 26-32.

Chapter 5

WOMEN'S ISSUES: RECOVERING YOUR VISION

M. Carolyn Thomas

Freedom of choice and equality have meaning only when you have developed options and plotted life plans. Then you can exercise freedom to choose from options. This freedom is real only when you have developed a plan to regain your position and strength. Developing plans and exercising options are the elements of freedom and autonomy, and the use of this freedom results in the reestablishment of meaning.

If you are a battered woman, mother of abused children, a displaced homemaker, or adult survivor of sexual abuse, you probably lost options that were once part of your vision for a meaningful life. Women who are victimized or who gradually or suddenly experience the loss of their support system generally feel isolated, abandoned, helpless, and powerless. Meaning in life and visions for the future are often either lost or so drastically changed that the women have little hope of ever regaining control of their lives. Education is a choice that can empower women who have experienced diminished emotional, social, or economic strength because of traumatic events that changed their life plans. If you are victimized or have experienced the loss of your support system, you can recover your vision by choosing an educational plan designed to restore your emotional, social, and economic strength.

Are You a Battered Woman?

　　Rebuilding your life can be a complex process if you are a battered woman. The experience of being battered is different for each woman, and most battered women adjust to their victimization in their own individual and unique way. However, most battered women share common behavioral and emotional effects, and progress through a series of similar response patterns before learning to escape the cycle of violence. These responses include shock, guilt, self-blame, shame, fear, helplessness, depression, low self-esteem, grief, a sense of little control over life, minimizing the battering, and anger. You may return to school after successfully escaping the cycle of violence, or you may enter school while still working your way through the adaptive response pattern. Your efforts to leave home may be ineffective and your requests for help may be denied. Your frustration and loneliness cycle you back into the relationship, more hopeless than ever, and the abuse continues. On the other hand, your efforts to break the cycle may be supported by family, friends, or agencies and you may find a new positive life.

　　Shock, Disbelief, and Denial - You rarely leave after the first episode of physical abuse because you have not gone through the cycle of tension building, abuse, and contrition. Your initial reaction is shock, disbelief, and denial. You do not recognize violence as a cyclical occurrence that is the problem of the abuser. You probably internalize the abuse and see it as a result of something horrible you must have done. You look for reasons and often may find some small or insignificant imperfection that you try to change. You probably fail to realize that all people are imperfect and nothing you do should warrant violence.

　　Guilt, self-blame, and shame -　　You may spend time blaming yourself for the violence, believing you deserve it, and trying to change behaviors so that the abuser will not abuse you again. You may make numerous attempts to become a more devoted mate. You may not yet even realize that those attempts are futile and the violence will occur as long as your abuser has the problem. No change you make in yourself will stop the violence. Only an abuser can change the violence problem.

Disillusionment -   You may become very disillusioned after enduring several cycles of violence. You probably accept the blame, try harder to change something, but still the cycle repeats itself. Hopelessness may set in, and you begin to realize that nothing you do changes the pattern of abuse. You still may not recognize the problem as that of your mate. Instead, you may begin to incorrectly believe that you will never be good enough for someone to love.

Fear and terror - You may remain in the violent relationship through numerous cycles. Your abuser may become very dangerous, so fear becomes the dominant motivator in your response to the violence. You may fear for your life or for your children's safety. You may make many attempts to leave, but your efforts are blocked. These unsuccessful attempts to escape or to seek help result in increased abuse. Not trying may seem safer than trying to get out of the abusive relationship.

Learned helplessness, depression, and low self-esteem - When your attempts to protect yourself are consistently blocked, you probably reduce or completely stop escape efforts. You simply do not believe that you or anyone else can help you escape the cycle of violence. It would not be unusual for you to consider taking your own life because you see no other way out. You may seek help for your depression without letting the professional know that abuse is the real problem. Minimizing or denying the abuse to yourself and others enables the cycle to be repeated without intervention.

Leaving home and loneliness - You may leave home after the first abusive incident, but this is unusual because most women fail to see the cyclical and repetitive nature of spousal abuse. Several cycles are usually completed before most women realize the violence is not an isolated incident. When you do leave, safety relieves the fear, but loneliness often becomes so acute that you return. This loneliness is made worse by the fact you have probably become isolated from your support system.

Working out a new life and special cautions - The ideal solution is to seek help from appropriate sources and to receive the help needed to protect you and to help you escape the cycle of violence. This may not occur right away. You may succeed only after several ineffective attempts. The following suggestions may enable you to take the steps that will free you from the cycle of violence:

1. Learn to recognize that violence consists of three phases: tension building, physical battering, and contrition.

2. Realize you will probably go through this buildup, blow up, and honeymoon cycle several times before recognizing the pattern.

3. Understand that breaking the cycle is a process, and returning to the violent situation is not necessarily a failure, but a normal part of a progressive series of strengthening steps.

4. Believe that the violence is not your fault, but the abuser's problem. Nothing you do warrants abuse.

5. Identify the effective sources of help, which generally include a shelter or counseling program for battered women.

6. Remember your abuser requires help for the abuse problem, so do not be persuaded by superficial efforts by the abuser. Abusers who quit drinking still have an abuse problem, and abusers who become religious still need professional therapy.

7. Do not seek marriage or relationship counseling until the abuser has received professional help and has not abused for a minimum of three to six months. Couple counseling for the two of you before the abuse stops is dangerous to you.

8. Rebuild your support system so you can combat the loneliness and helplessness.

9.   Strengthen your parenting skills.   Remember you may have lost much of your parenting power, so you may need to learn a different set of skills.

10.   Examine your childhood experiences to see if you were a victim of abuse. If you were, work through the issues with a knowledgeable counselor.

11.   Get help in working through your anger and lack of trust. These feelings can be associated with ongoing impediments   with   friends,   family   members, colleagues, or intimate partners.

12.   Break the cycle of abuse by empowering yourself so that your children will not be victims and you will be less likely to choose another abuser as a life partner.

Empowering yourself through education - Education can be a major strategy for rebuilding your vision. If you are a battered woman, you have probably lost much of your financial and social support, you may have a very diminished sense of self-worth, and you may grieve for lost dreams and opportunities. School is an excellent source of friendships, career development, personal counseling, healthy social opportunities, organizational involvement, life planning, and job placement.

Are You an Adult Survivor of Sexual Abuse?

Becoming a survivor of childhood sexual abuse is a process with certain identifiable goals. To begin with, you probably have experienced three definite effects. First, you may blame yourself and think something must be terribly wrong with you for someone to have abused you in so degrading a manner. Second, you probably have believed, or still believe, that you are the only person you know who was ever sexually abused. Because sexual abuse is the best kept secret, few people know that approximately one of every three women and one of every six men have been sexually abused by a family member or someone close to the family. Third, you live two seemingly separate lives. Close friends are rare because you would have to tell them your secret. You live an outer life for the public and another inner life with your painful secret.

Because becoming a survivor is a process, you can embark on this journey while going to school. However, you will be working through several steps, and expert counseling from the college counseling center or a specialized community agency can facilitate the journey through the healing process while you concurrently pursue your education. Groups for adult survivors of sexual abuse are particularly effective.

Becoming a Survivor - The first step in becoming a survivor of sexual abuse is to realize it was not your fault. You must overcome self-blame. You were manipulated into cooperating, and nothing you could have done could have stopped it. You were a child without the power to say "no", and cooperating has no meaning when "no" was not an option. Neither was there anything wrong with you. You probably often ask the question, "Why me?" You were abused simply because you were there and available and not because of some bad trait or characteristic.

Overcoming self-blame, shame, and guilt is not something you can achieve in a short time. It may take several months or even a few years. You will know you have achieved this goal when you can say, "What happened to me was a crime." You will also be unlikely to keep your abuse a secret, because you no longer believe you have any responsibility for the abuse.

Because few people understand the nature of sexual abuse, persons may respond in two ways when you disclose the abuse. They may want to deny or minimize it and continue the secrecy, or they may blame you. Nonabusing parents may not understand and express anger at you for breaking the silence. Emotional or legal consequences of the abuse may be blamed on your disclosure rather than on the crime of the abuser. You must resolve post-disclosure guilt.

Assuming even a small amount of responsibility for the abuse will enable the abuser to re-offend, so breaking the silence and resolving the resultant guilt are important. Thinking of other children who may have to endure what you have experienced may help relieve much of the guilt.

Your abuser gained unhealthy power over you by using oppression, guilt, manipulation, sympathy, attention, seduction, or other psychological games. Even though the physical aspect of the abuse may have ceased, you may still be vulnerable to the games. You have to release yourself from the power of the abuser. Be aware that not even the death of the abuser releases you from the feelings of victimization. You must identify the favorite strategy of the abuser and stop your victim response. Generally, you are only able to do this after you have overcome self-blame and resolved post-disclosure guilt.

The issue of forgiveness is important in this step. Remember that what your abuser did to you is never okay. Your goal is to re-evaluate the relationship, not to forgive, if forgiving means you relieve the abuser from responsibility, or say it is acceptable to you.

Building self-esteem and power is important in overcoming abuse. Advancing your education can be very helpful in building self-esteem and power. You set goals, develop options, use your freedom to choose and pursue options, and decide how you want to grow. Success, support from your peers, encouragement from teachers, overcoming small failures, and increased financial capabilities all strengthen your sense of power over your life and improve how you feel about yourself.

The final step in breaking the cycle is to stop most of your learned victim behaviors. You know you are achieving this goal when you no longer believe you are abusable by intimate partners, parents, children, friends, colleagues, teachers, or strangers. You begin to be able to trust and resolve difficulties in intimacy. You choose nonabusers as friends and partners, and your children believe you when you say "No."

The "No-Wheel"

Breaking the cycle and becoming a survivor can be conceptualized as an image of a wheel. The spokes of the wheel are your feelings of confidence, self-worth, trust, security, love, and competence, all of which are attached to the hub, which is your ability to say "No" and have it stick. The rim of the wheel represents autonomy, or competent self-regulation and empowerment. You can experience the feelings represented by the spokes only if you can effectively say "No." Your autonomy is dependent upon these feelings. This pictorial image shows why the ability to say "No" is central to breaking the cycle of abuse.

To encourage yourself throughout your personal and educational journey, remember these suggestions for becoming a survivor:

1.   Be patient with the pace of healing. Remember that becoming a survivor is a process and not something that occurs at one point in time or as the result of a single insight.

2.   Break the silence. Because keeping the abuse a secret prevents you from becoming a survivor, it increases the probability that others will be abused.

3.   Choose wisely the person to whom you disclose your abuse. Trained professionals or a support group are good choices for initial disclosures. They will be less likely to mistakenly blame the victim.

4.   Understand sexual abuse and be tolerant of your unique method for coping. Everyone adapts differently.

5.   Learn about normal development and compare what you experienced with expected growth experiences. The age at which you were abused and the duration of the abuse elicit varying responses.

6.   Remind yourself that it is perfectly all right to be imperfect. A common effect of sexual abuse is self-abuse, and few realize one form of self-abuse is trying to be perfect. You may notice this while pursuing your education.

Are You the Nonabusing Parent of an Abused Child?

Nonabusing parents of abused children are also victims, and their unique concerns are rarely addressed. If nonabusing parents are mentioned, the purpose is often to blame them for not detecting the abuse or for allowing it to continue. Mothers of sexually abused children often say their lives are over, nothing they have done counts for anything, or they have lost all meaning and purpose in life.

If you are a nonabusing parent, one way of regaining purpose and personal power is through education. As you pursue your academic education and rebuild your life, you must accomplish specific tasks.

Your first reaction after discovering the abuse of your child, especially if the abuser is your life partner, is disbelief. You have to overcome your own denial. Recognizing abuse, particularly sexual abuse, is difficult. Remember, sexual abuse is the best kept secret. You have to know the signs to detect abuse. Children rarely tell you because they blame themselves. Hopefully, you can find books for nonabusing parents, or ask professionals to help you determine if your child is being abused. To an uninformed observer, abusers do not seem different from nonabusers.

Most parents think abuse is something that happens to other people's children. This is especially true when you care for the abuser. For example, it is particularly difficult for a mother to accept that her son has abused a daughter or another son. Issues associated with breaking through denial include rejecting the abuser, self-blame, feeling powerless to stop the abuse, and not knowing how to help the child. Education about abuse provides most of the answers, and support groups are particularly helpful.

Denial is closely associated with working through guilt. Once denial is overcome, your next question is "How could I have not known it was going on?" Guilt follows acceptance of the truth. Guilt is augmented by the fact that your abused child, your family and friends, and many others ask, "How could you not know?"

Constantly remind yourself that you were not the abuser. Though your child accepts blame, you accept blame, and society may blame both of you, the abuser is the only person responsible for the abuse. Perhaps situations occurred in which your actions provided opportunities for abuse, but had you known your child would be abused, you would undoubtedly have changed your actions. Children are abused while the nonabusing parent answers the telephone, goes grocery shopping, or visits a neighbor, yet that parent accepts blame for the abuse. Also remember that abusers generally disempower the nonabusing parent before beginning the abuse.

You must break the silence in order to stop the abuse and obtain appropriate help for your child. You are fortunate if there is a community agency that specializes in treating child abuse. Counselors trained specifically in child abuse can help you decide whom to tell and where to make the report. Should you decide to pursue prosecution, the agency may have an advocate who will provide emotional support while you work your way through the complex legal system.

While you must report the abuse to the local child protective agency, divorce, custody, and prosecution are choices you should discuss thoroughly. Decisions should be made only with full knowledge and counseling from informed professionals. Experiencing the legal system can be the most frightening and painful step in overcoming the effects of abuse.

The journey you take in rebuilding your self-esteem and power is almost identical to the path your abused child must travel. Learning to say "No", recognizing your own victim behaviors, becoming financially secure, escaping the power of the abuser, and becoming a survivor are all prerequisites to help your abused child.

Although your child will require professional help you too can serve as a healer for your abused child. You are probably the only person in a position to provide everyday help. Never assume your child has resolved the abuse because of silence. It is imperative that abused children revisit the trauma and achieve the goals mentioned earlier. In addition to obtaining specialized counseling, you can try to:

1. Remain nondefensive when your child gets angry with you. Abused children are often afraid of the abuser. Their anger and blame are consequently directed at you. Although painful, your child may blame you for years if you do not listen nondefensively.

2. Allow your child to talk about the abuse. Many nonabusing parents think listening once is sufficient. As children develop, their views of the abuse change to match the cognition of various developmental stages. Listening when the child is ready to talk helps the child heal.

3. Express your willingness to listen and then wait for the child to find the best time.

4. Do not be afraid to learn, plan, and utilize positive discipline for your child. Many nonabusing parents fail to set limits because of sympathy or guilt, which is potentially harmful for your child.

5. Build a support system for yourself. Your child needs a healthy example. If you isolate yourself because of shame or self-sacrifice, you may actually contribute to continued or future victimization of your child.

Are You a Displaced Homemaker?

Divorce or death of a life partner can temporarily destroy your life plan. If you have recently divorced or ended a long term relationship, you are probably experiencing feelings similar to those of someone whose life partner has died. The grieving stages of shock, denial, guilt, anger, depression, bargaining, and acceptance are the same for most losses, but you may have more trouble in some stages than others. Grief counseling is helpful. Sharing your feelings in a group with other persons who are working through loss can reduce personal pain and shorten healing time. Although most adults are familiar with the grieving process, some specific recommendations may facilitate your recovery.

Take the time to heal. Grieving is a process and has to occur over time. You may try to delay or avoid the process but this only increases the duration and degree of pain.

Heal at your own pace. People married for 50 years require years to grieve, whereas a person losing a five year relationship may require six months to a year. Although you do not want to get stuck in denial, depression, guilt, or any other grieving stage, you can avoid perpetuating intense pain by dealing with issues when you are ready, rather than forcing the process. No set period exists for grieving. Because it is an individual pattern, find what is comfortable but productive for you.

Watch your investments. Many people continue to invest love, goals, time, money, or anger in the lost relationship. An investment may be healing for a widow but detrimental for an abandoned mate. Letting go, anger, guilt, rejection, trust, loneliness, and self-concept are all complicated issues associated with decisions about investments. Talking to nonjudgmental friends or counselors can help you discriminate between productive and destructive investments.

Use creative arts to recover. Everyone can use poetry, prose, music, play, or art to find special avenues for loosening the thoughts and feelings associated with loss. Symbols discovered in creative expression become inanimate friends that share the burdens of hurt, rejection, betrayal, loneliness, dashed dreams, anger, depression, or fear. Using artistic forms helps us become our own healers.

Find alternate sources of meaning. When you lost your relationship, you lost an important source of meaning. You do not have to live in a vacuum until you are ready for another relationship. In fact, if you are devastated by your loss and are having difficulty successfully progressing through the grief process, you may have used your relationship disproportionately as a source of meaning.   Other sources include creating something, appreciating the beauty of nature, and transcending a great difficulty. Consequently, deciding on your path to recovery may provide meaning to substantially fill the void left by the lost relationship.

Build New Dreams

If someone tells you, "I hope your dreams come true," you probably feel lost because your dreams have been shattered. You might respond, "My dreams can never come true." You realize your old plans are no longer possible because of victimization or loss of a relationship. Hopefully, you have a wise friend who tells you, "Then go build new dreams."

Education can provide you with new dreams, and help rebuild your emotional, social, and economic power. You were not responsible for what happened to you, but you can assume responsibility for overcoming your hurts and losses. Your old vision for your life is no longer available to you, but education can be a quest for you to recover your vision and build new dreams.

PART III

Coping: Creating and Accepting Change

This part offers strategies and solutions for conditions existing prior to school or created by your return to school. Its three chapters pertain to techniques for overcoming some of the problems presented in Part II. These chapters are grouped together because they provide the "how to" information needed to put ideas into motion and to transform dreams into reality. Chapter 6 guides students in their process of seeking help, finding the right counselor, etc. Chapter 7 provides ways for the reader to reduce apprehension and anxiety that interfere with educational success. Anxiety may negatively affect a test score or prevent enrollment altogether. Special techniques for relieving stress and minimizing anxieties are expanded in Chapter 8. It provides practical, easily utilized methods that can be self-initiated.

This part begins with a short narrative concerning school related anxieties and how they were resolved.

BETTY'S STORY

I have faced many decisions throughout my life which have varied in importance and complexity. For me, the decision to go back to school was one of the hardest decisions I have ever had to make. It brought about hours of anxiety and nervousness which created some minor physical problems.

Though I had always wanted to go to college right out of high school, my father had other ideas. He wanted me to work for a year before going to school. Immediately after graduation, I found a job working as a legal secretary for eight attorneys in the Attorney General's office. I enjoyed working so much I did not want to quit after a year. I thoroughly enjoyed my job, every aspect of it -- the duties, the income, but probably most of all, the interaction with others. After the first couple of months, truthfully I forgot about school. I had been dating someone seriously for three years and, like many members of my generation, I was married by the age of 19. Any serious thoughts of going to school had been replaced by my new job and marriage.

My husband and I began night school at a local college when we were both 20. I had no idea what courses to take but decided perhaps I should take accounting; it would help me balance my checkbook at the very least. It sounded like a good idea at the time.

After failing the course, I felt like a failure (a good reason for quitting school). Another reason for not continuing school was that I was pregnant. This was a perfect excuse to drop out -- after all, you didn't see many pregnant college students in those days.

After one quarter, I had built a strong case for becoming a dropout. I forgot about my education as my husband had quit his job and was busy in school full time.

Not having a degree didn't really bother me until my husband joined the Air Force. When I overheard wives talking about their college days, I felt left out. Embarrassed to admit that I had not gone to college, I felt inferior to these women.

When we moved to San Antonio, Texas, I had been out of school for 18 years. A friend told me she was going back to school and suggested I go with her. She already had one year and needed only one more year for an associate degree. When I called the school to ask about admission procedures, I was told I would have to take an entrance test; however, after much discussion the school agreed to allow me to enroll on probation. After five months of internal turmoil, I finally made the decision to go for it! Those months had been filled with fear and anxiety.

The mere thought of going to school was frightening and brought on many bouts with my stomach. I sent for my high school transcript and made an appointment to talk to a counselor. I was so nervous I could hardly open my mouth. My voice quivered and my stomach was in knots. My friend and I went together to talk with the counselor. After discussing her schedule first, my friend left me alone to talk to the counselor about my schedule. The counselor was very nice, understanding, and helpful. I decided to take a computer course so I could use our home computer. At the suggestion of the counselor, I also enrolled in a typing course to increase my speed on the computer.

When I told my children that I was going to college, they thought it was a big joke. "Why bother at your age, Mom?" was their initial response. My husband went along with the idea but I felt he was not too crazy about it. While he never made any negative comments, he never made any positive comments either. I sensed he was worried about how our home life might be affected. Could I handle my wifely/motherly duties in addition to school? I think this was uppermost in his mind along with the concern about the strain my education would place on our marriage.

Once I started school I thoroughly enjoyed it! I studied hard and did quite well. The next semester I decided to take three courses; I had eased into the world of academe.

I vividly remember the first presentation I was required to make. The thought of standing up in front of all those students terrified me. I felt they would expect more from me because I was older. I broke out in a rash; my stomach was in knots; my voice quivered, and I was nauseous.

Fortunately, I had a very understanding instructor who took time to talk to me. He helped me through that presentation as well as several more. He allowed me to make my presentation in front of a few people, not the full class. When I finished, I felt only a slight relief. . . .and that relief was simply because it was over! Inside I was furious at myself for not being able to handle it. I went home and cried; those feelings stayed with me for days. I realize now the anxiety I felt before the presentation was much more stressful than the presentation itself. Also, I now know that I was not the only one terrified!

The challenges that were presented to me in my classes were frustrating at times. It had been 18 years since I had been in school. Some things that I should have known I just did not know or could not remember. Things were not coming back to me like I had thought they would. Having had no math in 18 years, algebra was Greek to me. When I was in high school, computer language had never been heard of -- could I learn it? My study skills were rusty as were my math, English, and writing skills.

I wanted to do well and excel! I wanted A's in my course work as well as in my wife/mother roles. I tried to maintain our household without any major adjustments. To me, being a good wife and mother meant having nourishing meals prepared, a clean house, car pooling my children, and still having an active social life with my husband. This worked fine during my first two years of college when I was taking a light course load. The big adjustment came about once I decided to pursue a degree and settled on a major.

Deciding on a major was a long, hard battle for me. One day I would lean toward business and the next day psychology. This went on for months. Not knowing what you want to be when you grow up is pretty scary, especially when you are 36 years old! After seeing four different counselors from the various disciplines in one day, I realized that my options at that point were very limited because all my courses would not transfer to another major. I had worked too hard to lose these credits so I made the decision to change my major from business to psychology. I wouldn't lose credits that way. While this decision released some of the tension I had been experiencing, it was only a temporary respite.

Because of my husband's career, we are forced to be very mobile. We were only scheduled to be in Montgomery for three years so I knew if I didn't take 20 to 25 hours a quarter, I would never finish my degree without transferring to another college and possibly losing credits. I put too much pressure on myself; I wanted to finish so I could go through the graduation ceremony. I became very organized and set my priorities. With six months left, I decided to put graduation at the top of my list. I knew what my goal was and I could see the light at the end of the tunnel! My goal was to earn my B.S. in psychology and to participate in the graduation ceremony with my family present. I experienced some guilt when there were no meals prepared or only hurried meals at best. I was forced to give up some things that I enjoyed -- a ride in the country with my husband, PTA meetings, and even sewing. I also faced dilemmas such as:

> Do I study for my test when one of my children needs me to help her study for her test?

> Do I accompany my husband when he has job-related social obligations or do I stay home to do my school work?

The longer I was in school the more support I received from my family. My three daughters assumed additional duties. The older two girls also helped by car pooling the youngest one. With their friends, they became a sounding board for my speeches! I'm not sure when my husband became more supportive. I really think it was a gradual process. It became evident to me during my last year of school, especially my last six months. Maybe it was because I was doing well or perhaps he too could see the light at the end of the tunnel. He helped with the housework and the meals. When possible, he helped the children with their homework; he attended their functions alone if I couldn't go. He did all this with never a complaint!

Graduation was such a thrill! To walk across the stage and receive my diploma was a wonderful feeling -- the successful culmination of a dream come true! At that moment I felt a sense of satisfaction and accomplishment. All the frustration, anxiety, and fear were behind me; I had done it . . . accomplished my long awaited goal! My family was so proud of me. I could see the excitement in my children's eyes that night. I feel that seeing their mother achieve her long awaited goal of graduating from college will inspire them to set, pursue, and achieve their highest dreams.

Chapter 6

FINDING AND INTEGRATING SUPPORT

Carolyn K. Long

Now that possible impediments to change have been identified in previous chapters, methods to deal with those impediments will be discussed. This chapter presents various strategies for removing the impediments and effecting positive change in your lives.

Removing impediments can be accomplished through the development of personal autonomy and self-esteem. Personal autonomy exists when you are in control of your life economically, emotionally, intellectually, and physically. Achieving autonomy means increasing self-definition in terms of behavior, values, attitudes, thinking, and feeling. In the process of achieving autonomy you eliminate the legacy of self-doubt, self-blame, fear and emotional dependence. This is not an easy task in a culture which has encouraged the economic and emotional dependence of women. In choosing autonomy as a goal, you are choosing to do things differently than you have done them in the past. And you are choosing to change long-standing patterns of attitudes and behavior. For example, a decision to return to school is a move towards economic and intellectual autonomy. While it is possible to accomplish this task alone, it is much easier when you have the support of others.

Finding Support

Finding support means finding other people who understand your wants and needs, who respect you as a person, who listen compassionately to your fears and concerns. When you feel supported, you feel understood, encouraged, and valued for the person that you are. Those who support you do not judge or criticize. They listen, understand, and encourage you in whatever changes you are attempting. If you are lucky, you already have supportive people in your lives. If you are not so lucky, it is time to find some of those people.

The people who are most likely to offer support are people who have experienced similar problems and experiences in their lives. Although no one can know exactly what another person's experience is like, most people relate well to others who have had similar experiences. Visit any children's playground and you will find mothers talking about their experiences in child-raising. Their common experiences bond them together. In the same way, people who share your experiences in attempting to achieve personal autonomy can relate to your problems and circumstances better than those who have not experienced it.

The value of support groups is finding a group of people who understand your problems. Perhaps for the first time you will feel accepted, understood, and not alone. You will be able to drop the weight of dealing with your problem alone, and accept that there are others dealing with similar experiences. You will look around the room and see people much like yourself and feel a part of the group. You may realize that these people are just like you and you would never have known it if you hadn't risked just a little. You may even feel that your problems are not quite so bad compared to others. Eventually you may even wonder why you waited so long.

In a more practical way, a support group can offer the opportunity of sharing other people's experiences as a guide for your own. There may be other group members who have successfully dealt with a similar problem and they may share it with you. You also may use the group as a sounding board for your problem solutions, and gather valuable feedback from others. You may have the opportunity to gather valuable information on other available resources or new ideas. All of these benefits are mutual because you are also able to offer something to the group as you become more comfortable. Support groups are really just people helping each other to grow and develop in ways they have chosen for themselves. So where do you find people who share in your vision of personal autonomy?

Discovering Community Support

Finding a community sponsored support group is a good way to begin your journey to personal autonomy and self-esteem. Almost all communities now offer some resources or support services for people going through personal change. To locate these groups look in the front of the telephone book which lists community service numbers. Most of the specific support services available in each community are listed there. Call and ask for information. If the support service you want is not listed, you can call some of the other agencies to inquire about the one you want. Often the people who staff community service agencies are aware of services that are available and not listed in the telephone book. Even if you have already achieved personal autonomy and a high degree of self-esteem, it is helpful to have a support group of other returning students. Many colleges and universities already have campus organizations and services which are of interest to returning students. Ask the personnel in the admissions office or the student affairs office. Or, you might contact the student government organization which is usually the agency responsible for chartering student organizations. If there isn't an organization for returning students, you might want to start one.

There are community support groups for people who suffer from the effects of alcoholism, narcotics addiction, eating disorders, sexual dysfunctions, chronic illness, domestic violence, rape and other crimes, divorce, sudden death of children, and many others. Some universities also have support group meetings on campus. To get specific information about these groups, such as meeting times and places, you may need to make several calls. If you live in a small town, you may need to go to a larger community in order to locate these groups. Or, if you are a real organizer, start your own group! The important thing is to take the first step and make the first call.

For some of you, this may be the most difficult step. When you are seriously contemplating a change in your life, the most usual reaction is to begin to argue against it within yourself. You may begin with a litany of thoughts about what others will think, or how weak you are that you can't do this alone, or how maybe tomorrow it will be better. And some of you may begin to think about imagined consequences such as being embarrassed if you see someone at a meeting that knows you or your family, or being too emotional and feeling out of control. Most of you who carry a legacy of self-doubt and shame from the past, have been keeping the secret of your hurt and pain for a very long time. The threat of revealing this by attending a meeting of a support group is overwhelming because it will be the first time you have admitted to yourself and/or to others that you are in pain, and that you do have problems. It means letting go of your mask of being OK, whatever that means to you. It means admitting to yourself that you are not as together as you would like to think. You may fear exposure and rejection. These are powerful feelings and they may prevent you from making that first call and reaching out for support.

If this is your difficulty, there are several things you can do to overcome some of these feelings. You can make the call and pretend that you are seeking this information for a friend. You do not have to give your name just to get information. If you cannot do this yet, then read books about your problem. The appendix of this volume contains the titles of current books which relate to most problems. These books are available in bookstores and in libraries. As you read these books remember that there are other people who have experienced your situation and have written about it in the hope that it will help you on your journey to personal autonomy. Some of the books are about personal experience, while others are more technical. Read as much as you can about your particular problem and become familiar with the effects and the ways to make changes. This may reduce your fear of exposure sufficiently to allow you to seek a support group.

The chapter on "Coping Skills" in this book also gives some techniques for dealing with repetitive, negative thoughts that may be helpful in reducing your fear of reaching out for support.

No matter what you do to prepare yourself, the first time you go to a meeting of a support group can be a very frightening experience if you have no idea what to expect. In the absence of correct information, you may construct your own expectations and they are likely to be more negative than positive. Acknowledge your fear, recognize that fear is normal in situations where we do not have complete information. Remind yourself that you don't have to continue if you don't like it. Allow yourself to make the decision after you have had the experience. Make positive self-statements to yourself, such as "Seeking support is a positive thing to do for myself." And then just do it.

What you are most likely to find in a support group is people just like you that have problems similar to yours. In most support groups you are not required to say anything. You can go and just sit and listen. No one will attack you for not contributing. You may feel like contributing, but if you don't that's OK. A minimum of six meetings is necessary to determine if the group is what you want. It takes most people that long to feel comfortable with the other people and the process. Even if you don't like it at first, try to attend at least six meetings before you decide if this is the group for you.

Organization of Groups

Support groups are organized in different ways. Some support groups are composed entirely of people who share similar problems. Because there is no professional as a leader, these groups are usually considered to be self-help groups. Alcoholics Anonymous would be one example of a self-help group. Self-help groups may be less threatening initially because there is no professional there. Other support groups are organized and maintained by a professional, such as a counselor or psychologist. These groups may be more formal and structured and you may be interviewed by the group leader prior to actually attending a meeting. Just as with the self-help groups, these groups are usually organized around a particular problem or topic such as incest, drug abuse, etc. If one group is not comfortable for you, find another.   Groups differ in their composition, their interactions, and their leaders. Do not give up just because the first experience is not exactly what you want.

Most support groups will have some basic guidelines concerning interaction. These may center around equality of sharing time, not interrupting, not giving advice, etc. Usually new members are given a copy of these guidelines at the first meeting. If you are not, you might ask if the group has any particular guidelines concerning the organization and operation. You also might ask if they have any particular literature about the group that you may read. Whatever helps you to feel comfortable and more like other members, do it.

Recently, support groups were organized for those whose loves ones were serving in Operation Desert Storm.   The recognition that such service forced significant changes in families and that these changes caused many problems was widespread. Although the problems may not have been as personally threatening as a problem like domestic abuse, it demonstrated the value in sharing our problems with others who understand. In the past, there was a greater reluctance to admit that there were problems, and it was more difficult to find support. It is gratifying to know that it is more acceptable in this culture to have problems and to talk about them with others.

Individual Counseling

If you still find yourself unable to go to a support group you might consider individual counseling. Also, you might go to individual counseling if the support group alone is not meeting all of your needs. If you have deep emotional issues with which to deal, individual counseling may be the answer. In most cases, some type of individual help combined with a support group is best. A decision to seek counseling is an individual one and is certainly an expression of personal autonomy. Many of the same negative feelings mentioned in connection with support groups may surface. The most important thing to remember is that recognizing you have a problem and seeking help to solve it is a more mature choice than continuing in the same old destructive patterns. You are making choices about your life and in this way are becoming more autonomous. You are choosing change, not stagnation.

In seeking an individual therapist, be an intelligent consumer. Just as you would not leave all your knowledge at home when you go shopping for groceries, do not leave it at home when you go shopping for a therapist. Unfortunately, many people think that looking in the Yellow Pages is the best way to find a counselor and then stick with the first one they find. Or, if their first experience is not comfortable, they assume that all mental health professionals are the same and they give up. This is not intelligent consumerism. Just as there are many brands of cereal in the grocery store, there are many brands of therapists. Just as you may have preferences in cereals, you may have preferences in therapists.

Psychiatrists, psychologists, counselors, and social workers are all licensed to practice various types of therapy. Psychiatrists are trained as medical doctors and are the only group named that can prescribe medication. The other groups of mental health professionals all receive advanced graduate education in their respective fields. Individual psychologists, counselors, and social workers typically offer different types of treatment depending on their training. Although these treatments are too numerous to describe in this volume, there are many books available on the subject and you are welcome to explore if you are interested. However, it is not necessary to understand all the types of treatment in order to be helped.

There are some basic guidelines to follow in choosing a therapist. Foremost, the therapist should be a trained professional. This eliminates most relatives and friends. One of the reasons for eliminating these groups is that a therapist should offer a safe, secure, confidential relationship. This is not possible with friends and relatives. To find a therapist, you can consult with friends and relatives concerning therapists they may know. You might call a university close to you and talk to a professor in the counseling department or the psychology department. You might call the mental health center and ask about a referral. You could call the licensing agencies for these various professions and request referral. Despite all of these possibilities, most people entering therapy rely on the recommendations of friends, relatives or former clients. That is fine, and a good place to start. But, if you are not comfortable with that therapist after several sessions, seek a referral. The most important ingredient in a therapeutic relationship is trust. If you do not trust your therapist, then you may need to see another therapist. Under no circumstances should any therapist ever initiate or participate in any type of sexual contact with a client. This violates the safety and security of the therapeutic relationship. If your therapist were to do this, you should report it to the professional licensing board and terminate therapy with that therapist immediately.

The principles concerning confidentiality should be explained to you by the therapist. The only circumstance under which a therapist could reveal anything about you (even the fact that you are in therapy) would be if you were an immediate danger to yourself or others. For all practical purposes, the confidentiality of the relationship is inviolate. This guarantees you the safety and security to tell the therapist whatever you want and no one will ever know.

A therapist should be non-judgmental. You should feel accepted for who you are. If you feel that a therapist is being judgmental, then discuss it with the therapist. If you are not able to resolve the issue, then find another therapist. You can discuss any issue with a therapist, and you should expect to be able to resolve issues concerning the therapeutic relationship. This is your therapy, you are paying for it and doing the work necessary to progress and it should be comfortable for you. This does not mean that every session will be wonderful or that you will leave every session feeling better. It does mean that you should feel some progress over time and that you should feel respected and allowed to progress at your own pace.

For additional information, I highly recommend <u>A Guide to Psychotherapy</u> by Dr. Gerald Amada (see Appendix A). In slightly over one hundred pages, Dr. Amada gives a thumbnail sketch of psychotherapy in nontechnical language, and answers the most frequently asked questions about therapy.

Reading for Growth

Self-help books can be a valuable source of information and can foster positive personal growth. The more you know the better informed you are, and the more change you can anticipate. It is through new and different information that your creativity is awakened, your motivation is increased, your understanding is enhanced. And ultimately, this information allows you to make choices that may be different from the ones you made in the past. If there is no new information on which to make decisions, you will continue in the same patterns. It is when you take in new information that you are challenged to grow and change.

Self-help books are written for the layperson and usually present the material in a manner which requires no particular skill except reading. Their purpose is to provide information and assistance to those who will invest the time and energy in their own recovery. These books can be a valuable addition to any type of therapy or they may be used by themselves. Most of them contain recommendations for activities you can do by yourself or with a trusted friend or group.

The information presented lets you know that you are not alone and that many other people have suffered with the same problem with which you are struggling. And information on how they coped and eventually overcame the problem is also valuable.

Self-help books may give you new ways of looking at old patterns or maybe identify patterns of which you were not aware in the past. It is this increased awareness that helps you identify areas of your life that need changing. There are so many self-help books now available that they are too numerous to mention in this chapter, but some of them are listed in the suggested readings in the appendix of this book. Many of these are available in libraries and bookstores.

Whatever your particular impediments to personal autonomy and self-esteem, there is help available. If you make the decision to change, and actively commit your time and energy to that change, it will come. Recovery from whatever problems you may be experiencing is possible. Many others have achieved recovery and you can too. The first step is the most difficult, and that is to make the decision to do it.

Recovering the Vision

Once you have eliminated the impediments to personal autonomy and self-esteem, you may want to begin making serious plans for your life. You will have already achieved some of your goals, and you will have learned valuable skills along the way. Letting those skills work for you to improve your situation is certainly worth consideration. One excellent way to improve your situation economically and intellectually is to further your education.

Education offers you some unique opportunities to develop autonomy and self-esteem. As a student, you will have many opportunities to act responsibly and be appropriately rewarded with success. You will experience many challenges and obstacles. Overcoming these will lead to self-esteem. The very process of education encourages you to think for yourself, to be autonomous and to exercise control of your life. Many returning students who were initially filled with negative thoughts about their competence, have experienced remarkable success in academic work. Success in academics usually leads to economic success in the larger culture and to personal autonomy. The more success you experience, the more you begin to have a positive view of yourself and your decision.

If you decide to seek education as one of your life goals, then you will need a plan. Although planning is often talked about, it is not done often enough. There are certain elements in planning which are very important. These are discussed below.

1. Setting realistic goals. The key here is self-knowledge. The more you know and understand yourself, the more clearly you can assess your potential, your motivation, your inner resources. That is not to say that you are always correct, however. Some women seriously underestimate their abilities and talents due to low self-esteem. If your friends are telling you to go back to school, but you are doubtful, maybe you should consider taking your friends' advice. At least consider giving it a try.

A goal is an end toward which you are willing to exert effort. You may want to set both long-term goals (those that will require more than one year to accomplish) and short-term goals (those that require less than a year to accomplish). For example, getting a college degree is a long-term goal, while taking a course in shorthand is a short-term goal. Short-term and long-term goals may be related. For example, you might take the course in shorthand in order to qualify for a better position at work, which will also give you extra income to attend college in the evenings. The short-term goal is part of your planning to achieve your long-term goal.

Goals should be written statements of the end you hope to achieve and the time you think it will take. Writing them down will help you to keep them in mind when you may be losing your motivation. It will also help you to keep them realistic. You might really want to be an astronaut, but if you are already 40 years old, and just starting college, it is not very realistic. In considering what is realistic, consider your specific gifts, your talents, your likes and dislikes. Then try to combine them into your long-term goal. For example, if you would like to own a small business, you might consider taking some business courses which would help you get started. If you enjoy children, you might consider teaching as a career. Be as specific as you can, but also realize that you may change your goal as you gain more information about yourself and your likes and dislikes.

If you are not sure exactly what you want to do, you can just jump in and take a few courses that seem interesting to you. Or visit the career development office of the university and ask for career information. Or visit the library and read about various career opportunities. You may decide to do this investigating before or after you enroll in classes, but you should definitely do it before deciding on a major area of study.

2. Assessing needs. This step involves organizing your thoughts concerning all of the needs associated with achieving your goals. You may need child care, financial assistance, transportation, a more suitable living arrangement. You may need more unscheduled time to devote to studying, assistance with any handicapping condition, or remedial education to get you prepared for college level work. Brainstorm this situation with others. Ask them to think of as many things as they can which they think you might need. If possible, locate other returning students and talk with them about what their needs were, particularly any they hadn't anticipated. Even things such as typing services for papers should be included. And if you are devoting all this time to education, who is going to mow the grass, feed the kids, pick up the dry cleaning, and do the grocery shopping? What needs will you have when you or someone in your family is ill? Who will keep the children on school holidays? Will you need extra time for studying during exams? Or extra time for getting together with other students in study groups? The more you are able to anticipate all of your possible needs, the better your plan will be.

3. Finding resources. Once your needs have been identified, you can begin working on finding the resources to meet those needs. If you need financial assistance, visit the financial aid office of the university and find out what is available for you. Visit the library and look for lists of scholarships. If you need child care, ask about the availability on campus. Ask for recommendations from friends about off-campus services. Ask relatives or neighbors about the possibility of child care when children are in the recuperative phases of illness. In Chapter 8 are some excellent suggestions concerning time management and how to do all the chores and still go to school. Remember, many people have done it and you can too!

4. Making alternative plans for chance factors. Always anticipate the unexpected and you won't be surprised. Suppose you have a flat tire on the way to school? Do you know how to

change it? Suppose your car has to go in the shop for a week?
Do you have alternate transportation? Is any available? Suppose
your babysitter doesn't show up or is sick? Do you have an
alternate plan? While these may be unlikely occurrences, you can
significantly reduce your stress level if you have some advance
plans to deal with these situations.

5. Implementing the plan. As time passes, you will
continue to gather more and more information concerning the
success of your plan. If the information is telling you that it is not
working, stop and re-evaluate. Figure out why it's not working
and change. Adopt new strategies. Maybe you haven't found a
reliable babysitter. Try a child-care center instead. Maybe you
are not able to find enough time to study. Try a cooperative child
care arrangement with another returning student to free up some
additional time without additional cost. Maybe your classes are
not what you expected. Consult with an advisor, or another
student. Pinpoint the problem as specifically as possible. For
example, it might be that you don't understand the material, or
can't follow the instructor, or lack the appropriate background.
Pinpointing the exact problem can point the way to a solution.
Find out what the alternatives are. Continue to re-evaluate the
plan every few weeks to make sure that you are making progress
towards your goals. Be open to new information concerning your
plan which will be valuable to you. Do not give up too easily on
a plan, but do not be too obstinate either. For example, suppose
you know that you need to get a GED before you try to enter
college. You plan to take the test after studying for about three
months. After two months, you realize that you have studied a
total of two hours and that was while you were half-watching
"Designing Women" on television. You re-commit to your plan,
but again find you are just not studying the material. Sounds like
it's time to change the plan! If you continue to attempt to study
on your own, you are unlikely to accomplish your goal.   So
consider a new tactic. Investigate to see if your community offers
any GED classes that meet at a time which is convenient for you.
Enroll in the classes and try that. If you find that you are not
able to make the classes, then maybe you need to re-evaluate your
commitment to further your education. Perhaps something else
is more in line with what you really want to do with your life.

Perhaps you have talents in art or music that are more to your liking and you really want to take advanced lessons in that. Use the information you get about yourself to your advantage, not to "beat yourself up" with self-defeating thoughts and judgments.

A New Beginning: The Pathways to Meaning

As you embark on your journey to achieving your goals, you will begin to feel that your life is no longer a reaction to circumstances around you, but that you have some control over your experiences. It becomes easier to concentrate on the possibility of future successes and to expend less energy on past failure. Letting go of the past is a freeing experience, it affords you the opportunity to begin again, each and every day if you want to. And as you begin each day anew, less and less burdened by the past, you find more and more meaning is added to your life. You feel invigorated by each new day and its promise of additional experiences along your journey. You welcome new challenges and opportunities that come along. And you really like the new person you have become. Other people may notice the difference. Friends may comment that you are more interesting or younger looking or just more pleasant to be around. You feel a sense of direction and it shows in every word and action. And no matter what direction you are moving in, it is yours. You own it and you take responsibility for it. And all of that adds depth and maturity to your life. You feel more confident in your ability to make decisions which are in your best interests. And you trust your decisions.

Many returning students undergo a transformation which is remarkable. Such a transformation is the result of work, planning, dedication, and perseverance. And the payoff is worth the effort. The sense of personal autonomy and self-esteem is freedom at its best. Free of the pain, and ready to live fully in the moment savoring every breath. To paraphrase the ad for a popular hair coloring, "You're worth it!" Good luck on your journey to those of you who decide to take the first step.

Chapter 7

COPING WITH SCHOOL-RELATED ANXIETIES

Eugenie Nickell

While earlier chapters discussed continuing or recurring conditions that interfere with one's educational efforts, this chapter focuses on anxieties that may emerge and be magnified by academic challenges. Perhaps you will be disappointed to discover you still suffer from test anxiety. Just as in high school, the mere mention of a test may alarm you excessively. This chapter addresses three typical anxieties affecting college students: speaking, test, and social anxiety. Though these fears are real and serious to the sufferer, usually with a little help, they can be overcome. Several techniques are offered to alleviate these anxieties.

The effects of anxiety can greatly affect your educational progress. Regardless of how well you comprehend the study skills suggested in Chapter 3, you are still working below your potential if you cannot put the skills into practice to complete an exam or speech for a satisfactory grade. Like many others, you may be handicapped by anxiety. Anxiety usually refers to specific neurological reactions culminating in what is commonly referred to as stress. According to the <u>Diagnostic and Statistical Manual</u> (DSM III-R, 1987), anxiety is "apprehension, tension, or uneasiness that stems from the anticipation of danger, which may be internal or external." For college students, anxiety may result in the inability to concentrate or in debilitating panic attacks. In some cases, anxiety can be "situation specific," occurring only during tests, presentations, or in social interactions. Interestingly, anxiety may be both the cause and/or the consequence of problems. For instance, you may be anxious about an upcoming test so you put off studying for the test until the last minute. Does that sound familiar? The result or consequence of this procrastination is a low test score. This unsatisfactory performance increases your anxiety about the next test. This same scenario could occur with speech anxiety. Because of anxiety about speaking before a group, you avoid even thinking about the assignment. You, therefore, under-prepare which results in a poor presentation, again increasing future anxiety.

While a certain level of anxiety can be advantageous, too much anxiety can interfere and become truly troublesome. If you constantly contend with a fairly high level of general anxiety, even a slight anxiety increase can be debilitating. Monitor your everyday anxiety level and attempt to decrease it. Based on knowledge of yourself, you can recognize changes in your anxiety level. Understanding your physiological or behavioral responses to anxiety will alert you to changes. Intense reactions can limit your potential as a student as well as seriously impact your career. Time spent in school should be spent in acquiring knowledge, developing understanding, and practicing new skills which will enhance your marketability. Learning about anxiety, understanding how it can be destructive, and practicing techniques to reduce it should be included in your educational growth.

While reactions to stress vary, anxiety is generally manifested in three ways: physiological, cognitive, or behavioral. Examples of physiological reactions include: interneural (perceptual disturbances); neurovascular (hypertension, headaches, and cramps); neuromuscular (diseases of the joints, tense muscles, and headaches); neurohormonal (elevated levels of cortisol, increased blood pressure, and skin eruptions); gastrointestinal (upset stomach, heartburn, bloating, and ulcerative colitis); and respiratory (hyperventilation and asthma).

Examples of cognitive reactions include: forgetfulness, inability to concentrate, and the use of defense mechanisms which provide some temporary relief. Often these techniques are self-deceiving and minimize or mask the unpleasantness of stress. They are tricks we play on ourselves to avoid facing the causes of stress. A few of the more common defense mechanisms include:

1.   denial - refusing to acknowledge the situation or being emotionally dishonest;

2.   displacement - venting negative feelings toward other sources with reactions including anger at self or others, behaving vindictively and irritably;

3.   rationalization - creating excuses or fabricating reasons to explain situations rather than facing the obvious reasons for the stress; and

4.   repression - forcing stressful situations from the mind and being unable to remember them.

Behavioral reactions to stress include: avoidance, isolation, withdrawal, failure to finish projects, an increase in drinking and/or smoking, and attempting suicide. Probably one of the most common reactions to anxiety is avoidance which is an escape from the discomfort from our reactions to anxiety. One easy way to rid yourself of the clammy palms, hot flashes, dry mouth, and quivering voice is to just give up. Don't make the presentation or take the test. This is an option selected by many: they drop a letter grade, drop the course, or some even drop out of school completely.

Understanding how excessive stress can interfere with success and how to minimize this interference requires that you develop coping systems. Because social anxiety, speaking anxiety, and test anxiety are so important to students, this chapter will focus on them and offer strategies for coping with them. All three anxieties are particularly detrimental to educational advancement as well as career success. Remember, however, the coping techniques that are discussed later can be adapted to reducing or resolving other anxieties that affect you personally.

Social Anxiety

Often seen on college campuses as well as in the general population, shyness is a generalized social fear experienced by the vast majority. Zimbardo (1978) has studied shyness extensively. His surveys show that 80% of us report that, at some time in our life, we were shy. Over half of the respondents indicated continuing shyness. Shyness results from discomfort experienced when one interacts socially. Anxiety produced as a consequence of shyness is called social anxiety. According to Buss (1980), shyness is just one reaction to social anxiety. He also includes embarrassment, shame, and audience anxiety, any one of which can cause discomfort.

As with other anxieties, social anxiety is manifested in rapid breathing, a rise in blood pressure, heart racing and pounding -- all brought about by the sympathetic division of the autonomic nervous system. Meeting new people, beginning a new career (such as returning to school), accepting a promotion, and conspicuousness (being the only "non-traditional" student in a classroom) are all examples of situations that can produce social anxiety.

Perhaps one of the most serious consequences of social anxiety is the overwhelming desire to escape or to avoid particular situations. Much energy and time may be channelled into devising elaborate schemes for avoidance. Have you ever been at a social event where you were asked to tell your name and something about yourself? Did you excuse yourself or maybe you stayed -- rehearsing what you were going to say over and over in your mind, all the while suffering extreme discomfort? Have you ever been invited to a dinner party and found yourself seated next to a stranger? How did you feel and what were you thinking?

Frequently non-traditional students enter academia exhibiting withdrawal, shyness, and low self-esteem. Sometimes this is quite obvious in the classroom -- an "older" student sitting off to the side, away from the younger students. What about these students, young or old, who want to ask a question during class but the very thought creates discomfort? They don't dare open their mouth, a common dilemma for shy students. The avoidance behavior of individuals who suffer from social anxiety often perpetuates other problems. Their tendency to withdraw and present themselves in a passive manner prevents job opportunities an meeting new friends.

Speaking Anxiety

There are several definitions of speaking anxiety. According to Paul (1966), speaking anxiety is the level of fear or anxiety that a person perceives by either anticipating a presentation or speaking to a group. McCroskey (1978), on the other hand, believes that speaking to a group is just one component of this type anxiety. His components include: speaking one on one, speaking to a small group, speaking to a larger group, and finally public speaking. In any case, regardless of the audience size, the anxiety is real. Students who experience speaking anxiety find themselves dropping classes that require presentations, no matter how large or small the requirement. If they continue the course, they may take grade reductions to avoid presentations.

The anxious behavior of individuals with speaking anxiety is manifested in various ways. Arnold Buss (1980) breaks the observable features into three categories: expressive, physiological, and instrumental. Because you are standing in front of the audience, the expressive component is obvious: quivering voice, erratic or poor eye contact, frightened or even petrified look, and paleness. The physiological component, as mentioned before, consists of sweating, increased blood pressure, pounding or rapidly beating heart, and rapid breathing. Last, the instrumental element, which is also easily observed, appears as disorganization. A nervous laugh, fumbling of papers, stammering, blocking, and loss of place occur as fear is intensified. This intensity causes many speakers to cut their presentations short or speed up, talking too fast to be understood, both resulting in a poorer performance.

Many students are concerned about exhibiting anxiety during a presentation. Research findings suggest that untrained audiences, like those in a college classroom, are not very aware of speaking anxiety (Behnke, Sawyer, and King, 1987). Instead, the students are probably focusing on what they have to present -- not what the speaker is presenting. McCroskey believes that a student giving a presentation in class for a grade is more anxious than if the student were giving the same presentation in a less formal setting, such as the dorm. Similarly, when we conducted workshops for students with speaking anxiety, we found that speakers generally rate their level of anxiety much higher than their audience rates it.

Low self-esteem, shyness, and public self-awareness all play parts in audience or speaking anxiety. Individuals with low self-esteem have a tendency to worry more about speaking to a group. Shy individuals who become anxious socially also show concern when speaking in public (Buss, 1980).

Each time you successfully complete a presentation in class, you become less aware of your anxiety, probably because you feel less anxiety. This does not occur all at once but over time. Do not anticipate losing all your anxiety, for as stated before, some anxiety helps to keep us alert and enthusiastic. With practice, you will become more relaxed and uninhibited and, therefore, better able to concentrate on your presentation.

Test Anxiety

Test anxiety is defined as apprehension or uneasiness stemming from the anticipation or fear of taking tests. It is often characterized by low academic performance, irrational thoughts, an increase in physiological arousal, inadequate study habits, and poor coping skills. According to Spielberger and associates (1970), a moderate amount of anxiety can actually facilitate test performance. In other words, to be effective we need to experience some anxiety. It is when we exhibit excessive anxiety that it interferes with and creates discrepancies in our performance.

Liebert and Morris (1967) suggest that there are two identifiable elements to test anxiety. The first is the cognitive element or worry which is expressed through thinking about the consequences of failure or displaying doubts about performance ability. The second element is emotional which refers to the physiological responses which are displayed during a testing situation. These responses include an increase in pulse rate, accelerated heart rate, and hot or cold flashes. Liebert and Morris found that dramatic emotional increases can occur as early as five days before a test or as late as the period before the test. This emotion decreases at the same rate immediately after the test.

Highly test-anxious individuals perform poorly because they are unable to focus on the task at hand. Instead their attention becomes focused on their discomfort. They worry about how well they are doing or how well others are doing; they ruminate about their performance, and they are repetitive in their method of solving the tasks. Because of their inability to focus, test-anxious individuals perform poorly on difficult tests. In comparison, low test-anxious individuals direct their attention more at the task at hand -- the test (Wine, 1971).

Remedies

If you experience social, speaking, or test anxiety, there are several useful methods to help you reduce your disturbing reactions. Progressive relaxation, systematic desensitization, deep breathing exercises, positive imagery, cognitive restructuring, and assertiveness training are all useful techniques for coping with anxieties. In the following discussion, these strategies will be explained and related to the particular anxiety they seem to work best with. To learn more about the ones that interest you, visit the university counseling center and the library. Special workshops and detailed literature are readily available.

Progressive Relaxation and Systematic Desensitization. This is a technique used to combat most anxieties and has proven to be very beneficial. Studies by Paul (1969) show that deep muscle relaxation causes reactions which are in direct contrast to anxiety's effects. By practicing deep muscle relaxation on a regular basis, you can decrease the anxiety caused by stressful situations.

Maladaptive anxiety can be weakened by systematic desensitization, a method to decrease anxiety-response habits in a step by step manner.   Both progressive relaxation and systematic desensitization are explained in more detail in Chapter 8.

Deep Breathing. A simple technique but one which works well for most types of anxiety, deep breathing can be done while riding in the car, standing in the grocery line, or while walking into a room full of unfamiliar faces. You begin by taking a deep breath and holding it for approximately 7 to 10 seconds before exhaling it through your mouth. This procedures is repeated several times. As you exhale, you feel the tension leaving your body.

Positive Imagery. Your images about success can become reality when you practice putting together positive scenes. These scenes are mental pictures or "make believe" stories involving you in difficult situations. Visualize or imagine yourself in an anxious situation and responding in the desired manner. Do this while training your body to relax and soon you'll discover that you will be more relaxed when you're actually in the anxiety-provoking situation. Begin by settling into a comfortable chair in a dimly lit room free of stimuli. Close your eyes and involve your senses in the image you want to create.   Imagine yourself responding appropriately in a specific situation. For instance, if you have difficulty meeting people, your image should be a clear visualization of yourself interacting socially with new acquaintances -- free of undue stress!

There are many methods for applying positive imagery or visualization. The Relaxation and Stress Reduction Workbook (Davis, Eshelman, and McKay) describe eye relaxation, metaphorical images, and creating your own special fantasies as imagery techniques to reduce anxiety. As with any of these remedies for controlling anxiety, you must practice on a daily basis.

Cognitive Restructuring. This technique focuses on your thought patterns and self-talk. It seems the information your mind processes either originates from without ourselves (often from significant others in our life) or from within (what we tell ourselves). You need not speak out loud to mentally talk to yourself. We often tell ourselves, "I shouldn't have done or said that. Next time, I'll . . . ." If you're thinking in terms such as "I can't," or "I'm just not able to," then you begin the task already strapped with a real burden. Look at the examples below:

Task #1	Others say "You can."	You tell yourself, "I can."
Task #2	Others say, "You cannot."	You tell yourself, "I can."
Task #3	Others say, "You can."	You tell yourself, "I cannot."
Task #4	Others say, "You cannot."	You tell yourself, "I cannot."

If you're attempting a new task, say Task #1, and you're hearing "you can" from others while saying "I can" to yourself, you probably complete this task in style. Task #2 should be no problem though others are saying you can't do it. Because you are saying "I can," your self-confidence will generally prevail. Do it and show them -- they will be less skeptical in the future. Research has shown that some of us are more controlled from without, what others tells us, while some of us are more controlled from within. This is referred to as "locus of control." Awareness as to which influences you the most would help in predicting your success on tasks #2 and #3. Tasks #3 and #4 are the most difficult. This is where learning to change your own self-talk becomes important. With practice at controlling your self-talk and by restructuring your thoughts, you can convert both tasks #3 and #4 into successful experiences. Obviously your completion of Task #4 is doubtful. It's hard to complete a task if you're telling yourself you can't do it while others are echoing this doubt.   Researchers   have   demonstrated   that   cognitive restructuring can be a very effective procedure. It takes concentrated practice to become aware of and to change your own self-talk. It involves: hearing what you are telling yourself; becoming aware of the negative thought; removing the negative terms; and replacing them with positive ones.

Assertiveness Training. At the same time you practice relaxation, deep breathing, and imagery, you can complement the results by learning more about assertiveness. Wolpe (1958) defines assertiveness as "expressing personal rights and feelings." Research shows that learning to be assertive is an effective means for changing your behavior, decreasing anxiety, and improving self-esteem. Through gradual controlled exposures, you allow yourself to engage in simple events that cause only minor discomfort. You should begin by learning how to respond in a non-threatening assertive way rather than in a passive way. There are many assertiveness techniques which you can practice.

The goal of assertiveness training is to increase assertive responses in various situations while at the same time decreasing passive or hostile responses. Most of us don't express ourselves the same way in all situations. We might be assertive with our loved ones but more passive with people we don't know. Ideally, we should be able to stand up to anyone for our rights in a non-hostile manner without violating their rights. Being able to express our feelings (likes or dislikes), being able to accept compliments graciously, or being able to say "no" enables us to feel more comfortable and relaxed as well as develop self-confidence and build self-esteem.

How would you react to the following scenarios?

1.   At your favorite restaurant, you order a rare steak. When it arrives, it is well done.

2.   You are in line at the grocery store and someone breaks in front of you.

How would you respond to these two situations? Would you be passive, aggressive, assertive, or would there be a response? You may be the type person that finds it difficult to express your feelings openly or respond to criticism. Being able to express yourself without blaming or threatening others can be achieved by using "I" instead of "you." "I disagree" instead of "You're wrong!" or "I like my meat rare" instead of "You must not hear good" or "I believe I was here before you" instead of "You get the hell out of my line" would be more appropriate. Using "I" integrates your feeling (like, disagree, or believe, etc.) with a particular behavior of the other person without attacking that person.

Another technique is to list specific situations where you feel you could be more assertive. In other words, take inventory. Keep a log of those times when you should have been more assertive and weren't, as well as those times when you acted assertively. Review this log weekly to evaluate improvements.

You can continue improving your assertiveness skills by reading more about assertiveness and by utilizing these skills in brief but controlled social contacts. Gradual exposure to simple situations can improve your overall social skills. Below are a few examples of how you can shape your behavior, gradually bringing about a more relaxed feeling in social situations:

1.   Speak first to a classmate.

2.   Compliment someone.

3.   Ask someone you don't know for directions.

4.   Strike up a conversation with someone in the campus cafeteria.

5.   Introduce yourself to a new person (Maybe the student sitting next to you in class).

Don't forget to monitor or evaluate your level of discomfort to see what's working for you. Give yourself recognition or reinforcement by awarding yourself points for each assertive response. When you've earned five points, reward yourself with a movie, a slice of pie, a new belt or scarf, etc. You will feel good about yourself and your self-confidence will grow as you become a more assertive person. As with any skill, being more assertive requires practice. It may feel awkward at first, but as it becomes a part of your repertoire, you will see your self-confidence improve and your discomfort or anxiety diminish.

Putting the Theories into Practice

Most returning students readily admit to suffering from some anxieties. The more you know about yourself, the easier it will be for you to identify personal anxieties. Each of the remedies discussed is easily utilized in dealing with social discomfort. Deep breathing before and during a social event may be all you need. For someone else, assertiveness training may enable them to cope with social anxieties. One or more of these techniques will prove applicable to practically any anxiety you have.

Literature shows a multifaceted approach is most successful in coping with speaking anxiety. Systematic desensitization, progressive relaxation, deep breathing, imagery, and cognitive restructuring can be incorporated in efforts to overcome or cope with speaking anxiety. You may want to experiment with specific approaches and find the ones that are most effective for you.

Test anxiety decreases as a result of a combination of behavior/cognitive remedies. Again, all the techniques are effective for test anxiety but we refer you to Chapter 8 for more discussion on test anxiety. Additionally, you should find that the study skills presented in Chapter 3 enable you to be better prepared for exams which will increase your self-confidence to do well on exams.

One final note about your level of anxieties concerns your overall health. Researchers such as Bagley (1981) have found poor nutritional habits are common for college students, especially those with emotional complaints and behavioral problems. Always being on the go and generally being behind on reading and projects translate into marginal health. Increasing the negative effects of anxiety, these conditions allow stress to take a greater toll. Another generality is that college students don't get the exercise they need. When you return to school, you may find yourself in life's fast lane which appears to be a hyper-pace that is not conducive to good health. As you practice the techniques for stress management, also be aware of your general health. Make necessary adjustments to ensure adequate nutrition and exercise.

All of these remedies are easily utilized in dealing with anxieties. None are really complicated and more literature is readily available if you want to research a particular approach more thoroughly. You may want to try each of the techniques to determine the ones you are most comfortable with. Combine as many as you want, but remember to practice them and utilize them if you sense your anxiety level increasing.

Conclusion

This chapter has condensed a lot of information supported by good research. It should prove useful to you, the returning student, in your academic efforts, but you will enjoy the benefits of learning to cope with anxiety in other areas of your life as well. If a certain anxiety continues to create discomfort for you, we suggest you seek more information. The counseling center is a free service and the library is a great resource for these topics. Some professors are very understanding and helpful in response to your interest in professional development and desire for self-improvement. By removing obstacles that prevent you from attaining your full potential, your education should prepare you for advancement and fulfillment, both personally and professionally.

References

American Psychiatric Association (1987) <u>Diagnostic and Statistical Manual of Mental Disorders.</u> (3rd ed.) Washington DC: APA.

Behnke, Ralph R., Sawyer, Chris R. & King, Paul E. (1987) The Communication of Public Speaking Anxiety. <u>Communication Education</u>, 36, April, 138-141.

Buss, Arnold H. (1980) Self Consciousness and Social Anxiety. San Francisco: W. H. Freeman.

Davis, Martha, Eshelman, Elizabeth, and McKay, Mathew (1988) <u>The Relaxation and Stress Reduction Workbook.</u> Oakland: New Harbinger.

Bagley, R. (1981) Relationship of Diet to Physical/Emotional Complaints and Behavioral Problems Reported by Women Students. <u>Journal of Orthomolecular Psychiatry</u>, 10, 284-298.

Liebert, Robert and Morris, Larry (1967) Cognitive and emotional componenets of test anxiety: A distinction and some initial data. <u>Psychological Reports</u>, 20, 975-978.

McCroskey, J. C. (1978) Validity of the PRCA as an index of oral communication apprehension. <u>Communication Monographs</u>, 45, 192-203.

Paul, G. L. (1966) <u>Insight Versus Desensitization in Psychotherapy</u>. Stanford, CA.: Stanford University Press.

Paul, G. L. (1969) Physiological effects of relaxation training and hypnotic suggestion. <u>Journal of Abnormal Psychology</u>. 74, 425.

Spielberger, C. D., Gorsuch, R. L. and Lushene, R. E. (1970) <u>Manual for the State-Trait Anxiety Inventory</u>. Palo Alto: Consulting Psychologists Press.

Wine, J. (1971) Test anxiety and the direction of attention. Psychological Bulletin, 76, 92-104.

Wolpe, Joseph (1958) Psychotherapy by Reciprocal Inhibition. Stanford, CA.: Stanford University Press.

Zimbardo, Phillip (1978) Shyness. Reading, MA: Addison-Wesley.

Chapter 8

COPING WITH CHANGE

Carolyn K. Long and Eugenie Nickell

Returning students are usually highly motivated to succeed and have heavily invested their resources in this success. The re-entrance into academic work demands that they adapt, cope, or adjust to this new environment. These demands on the students qualify as stress, as defined by Hans Selye (1976), a noted researcher in this field. The reactions to stress can be mental, physical, or both. The mental reactions to stress include doubts about competence and ability, fear of failure or fear of success, and fear of the unknown. The physical responses to stress include physiological reactions that are usually labeled anxiety. These reactions include, but are not limited to, shortness of breath, rapid heartbeat, rapid breathing, sweaty palms, obsessive thoughts, "butterflies" in the stomach, stomach aches, and diarrhea. The physical manifestations of anxiety reactions can be very mild or quite severe, depending on the situation and the individual. These are the same responses you might feel if you were being threatened. In one sense, considering a return to school is a threat. It is a psychological threat to your sense of well-being, and it can produce physiological symptoms which are labeled anxiety and/or fear.

Situations which are new or at least, unfamiliar cause you to doubt your ability to succeed and lead to stress. In addition, as a non-traditional student you may tend to increase stress by having high expectations about your performance. Because you frequently don't know what to expect, you can feel paralyzed by the fear, controlled by the circumstances, and generally overwhelmed. Thoughts about the various circumstances in which you may find yourself often result in feelings of inadequacy, self-doubt, and fear. These feelings then direct behavior in ways which are at best nonproductive and, at worst, counterproductive.

For example, imagine that you are faced with an examination on Friday. On Monday you begin to study, but you are anxious and nervous about learning the material and remembering it on the exam. You may be plagued with thoughts of "I'll never learn all this material" or "I'll never be able to remember all of this." These thoughts increase your anxiety and fear and further interfere with your study behavior and test performance. You find yourself unable to perform on the test at your expected level, and you receive a low grade. Some students would use this information as evidence that they made the wrong choice about returning to school. They might conclude that dropping out is the best thing to do. So they leave school discouraged and disappointed. In their own minds, they have confirmed their suspicions that they really didn't have what it takes to succeed. This negative experience also reduces their willingness to take risks in the future.

The problem with this scenario is that they really didn't have the opportunity to find out if they have what it takes to succeed. They lacked the coping skills to deal with the unfamiliar situation and the thoughts and feelings which interfered with their performance. It is the lack of coping skills which led to the failure. One of the tasks required for a successful return to school is learning to manage the anxiety and fear in a positive way. Fortunately, there are coping skills which can aid tremendously in reducing the stress which results from these self-defeating thoughts and feelings. This chapter will discuss some of those techniques which are relatively simple and easy to learn and use.

Relaxation

People who practice some form of relaxation are less tense, less anxious, and are more able to resist the negative consequences of stress. They report feeling happier, more optimistic, more energetic, and frequently display greater self-confidence. By learning to completely relax your body when you are not in a stressful situation, you will be able to carry this skill into stressful situations and reduce the level of anxiety you feel. In addition, the positive effects of relaxation will carry over into your everyday life, resulting in an overall reduction in anxiety and fear. This will give you more available energy to try new activities, such as returning to school, losing weight, exercising, etc.

Each person is unique and therefore their methods of relaxation may vary. For some, relaxation may be the result of vigorous physical activity such as tennis, swimming, dancing, or running. For others, relaxation may be a result of very limited activity such as watching TV, soaking in the bathtub, or reading. Just to alleviate the daily stressors in your life, it is wise to incorporate some form of relaxation into your schedule each and every day. This can also help to minimize your reactions to everyday frustrations and stressors and help you to rediscover some of the simpler pleasures in life. There is plenty of evidence that relaxation is healthful and beneficial to your heart. But, if you are planning to return to school, you will be faced with even more daily stressors than you are probably experiencing now, stressors such as anxiety and fear. To successfully manage these feelings and situations, you may need more specific techniques such as those described in this chapter.

Progressive Relaxation

Progressive relaxation was developed by Dr. Edmund Jacobson in 1938 and modified by Wolpe in 1958. This form of relaxation reduces the pulse rate, respiratory rate, and blood pressure and focuses on the four major muscle groups: 1) hands and arms; 2) head, neck and shoulders; 3) chest, stomach, and lower back; and 4) legs and feet. The basic technique consists of tightening and relaxing each of these muscle groups while focusing on the feeling of the muscle, both when it is tense and when it is completely relaxed.

The ultimate goal of progressive relaxation is to learn to relax tense muscles at any time.   Dr. Thomas Borkovec, a psychologist at Pennsylvania State University, reports that after sufficient practice most individuals are able to relax their bodies within five minutes. Although the amount of tension which is present in our daily lives differs, Borkovec says that most people have reached some adaptation level of tension with which they are able to function. Many times when you think you are completely relaxed, you are probably still moderately tense, and progressive relaxation can help you learn the difference between these states.

Dr. Dean Ornish, director of Preventive Medicine Research in San Francisco, has shown that training in progressive relaxation, as part of a lifestyle change, has positive effects. It not only decreases cholesterol levels but also increases the flow of blood to the hearts of those suffering from obstructive coronary heart disease. Relaxation has also helped those with diabetes, asthma, and acute pain. If it can do all this for those who have serious physical problems, imagine what it can do for you!

Before you begin to learn the actual technique, find a special place which is comfortable for you. Perhaps a seldom used room with a comfortable chair is available. Dim the lights or draw the curtains to eliminate as many outside distractions as possible. Sit erect in the chair with your feet flat on the floor and your eyes closed. You are now ready to begin!

First, take a deep breath through your nose, and hold it for about five seconds, and then completely exhale this breath very slowly through your mouth. Repeat this step four or five times. Concentrate on your breathing. As you inhale, feel the cool air rushing into your lungs. As you exhale, feel the warm breath as it passes through your mouth. Eliminate all other thoughts from your mind and concentrate totally on your breathing.

Second, concentrate on your hands, forearms, and upper arms. Tense and contract these muscles by making a tight fist.

Hold the fist for at least 10 seconds while you concentrate on the feeling of tension in the muscles.

Third, gradually relax your fists and feel the muscles relax. When your fists are completely relaxed, concentrate on the feeling in these muscles. Compare the tense state with the relaxed state. This allows you to focus on complete muscle relaxation.

Fourth, contract and tense the muscles of your head, neck, and shoulders by raising your shoulders and trying to bury your head in them. At the same time, contract the muscles of your face by squinting your eyes and making a funny face. Don't be embarrassed; you are alone and no one can see. Hold this position for about ten seconds and concentrate on the feeling of tension.

Fifth, gradually relax your shoulders and face. When you are completely relaxed, concentrate on the feeling in the muscles. In your mind, compare this feeling to the feeling of tension.

Sixth, contract the muscles of your abdomen and lower back by tightening your stomach muscles - "suck it in" as they say in the army! At the same time, contract the muscles in your buttocks. This should raise you up in your chair. As with the other muscle groups, hold this tension for about ten seconds and then gradually release it. When the tension is completely released, concentrate on the feeling of relaxation in the muscle.

Seventh, repeat the procedure with the final muscle group, the legs and feet. You can do this by trying to press your feet through the floor and really putting all of your weight into them while remaining seated. Hold this position for about ten seconds and concentrate on the tension in the muscles. Now, gradually release the tension. When the muscles are completely relaxed, concentrate on the feeling of relaxation.

Now focus your attention on the various body parts, checking for any remaining muscle tension. If there is an area that is not completely relaxed, repeat the procedure for that area. Most people have some body areas that are more difficult to relax than others, and you may have to use the procedure more than once on these areas.

Your body should now be completely relaxed. Sit there for a few minutes and enjoy the feeling. Breathe deeply and concentrate on your breathing. Let go of all your cares and concerns for this moment in time and just enjoy.

Whenever you feel completely relaxed and comfortable, gradually and slowly open your eyes. You should feel relaxed, refreshed, and much less tense.

This entire sequence can be done in 10-15 minutes and should be practiced at least twice a day. Relaxation is a skill, and like all skills, it must be practiced to achieve the maximum effect. After two or three weeks, you should be able to recognize almost immediately when you are tense and your muscles are not completely relaxed. With sufficient practice, you should be able to completely relax. If you are not successful in achieving complete relaxation on your own, there are many audiotapes available in most local bookstores to help you learn this skill.

Once you have mastered the technique, you are ready to apply it to real life situations. Suppose you are ready to start studying for your first examination. Take a few minutes to completely relax and clear your body of all tension. As you are studying, take relaxation breaks and repeat the procedure. And just before the examination, do the relaxation procedure again. Combined with the other techniques which follow, this should help you remain relaxed and allow you to perform at your peak.

Autogenic Suggestion

Another method of achieving deep relaxation was developed by Johannes Schultz in 1959. The theory behind autogenic suggestion is that the mind controls the body, forcing it to relax. This is done by focusing on feelings of warmth and heaviness. As with progressive relaxation, warmth and heaviness are signals that the body is totally relaxed. Richard R. Bootzin, Ph.D., states that, through this mental suggestion, the feelings of heaviness and warmth result in "a state of low physiological arousal."

To facilitate autogenic training, Beata Jencks, a psychologist, suggests that you imagine yourself as a Raggedy Ann doll. Sit in a comfortable chair with your eyes closed to experience a feeling of heaviness. Begin by lifting one arm a little and then letting it drop. Think of your arm as if it were the arm of a Raggedy Ann doll, completely limp. Feel the heaviness as it falls. Lift the other arm and feel the heaviness. Concentrate on the downward force of gravity and the feelings of heaviness. As you experience the heaviness, think of complete relaxation.

Another way to experience the feeling of heaviness is to think of a slinky sitting on the top of a stairway. Your head is the top of the slinky. Close your eyes and imagine the slinky slowly going down the steps. Feel the heaviness as it drops from your head to your toes.

To experience the feelings of warmth, imagine that you are a floppy doll lying in the sun with the sun's rays warming you. Your body is warm, but your head is cool. Concentrate on the feelings of warmth in the various parts of your body, legs, feet, arms, and hands. As you concentrate on this warmth, feel the relaxation of the muscles in your body. Continue this imaginal exercise until you feel completely relaxed.

Systematic Desensitization

Systematic desensitization, although its name sounds forbidding, has helped many individuals learn to decrease anxiety in specific situations. Developed by Joseph Wolpe in 1969, it has been shown to be highly effective. The technique consists of three stages: 1) learning deep muscle relaxation; 2) developing a hierarchical scale of anxiety-producing scenes; and 3) pairing the relaxation with anxiety-reducing scenes. Theoretically, the relaxation response is incompatible with the anxiety response because you cannot feel anxious and relaxed at the same time.

In the first stage, use the previously described methods of obtaining deep muscle relaxation. This will reduce your pulse and respiration rates as well as your blood pressure, and allow you to become completely relaxed.

Now that you have mastered the relaxation response, construct a list of things which arouse anxiety in you. Arrange them in order of the degree of anxiety they arouse. Begin by listing your least disturbing scene. In the case of a student taking an examination, she might list seeing a test date on the course description as the least anxiety-producing. The next least disturbing scene, such as having the teacher announce the test date, would follow. This process would continue until she has listed all the anxiety-producing scenes associated with taking a test. An example of a list for the test taking situation is shown below.

1. Seeing the test date on the course description.
2. Having the teacher announce the first test.
3. Receiving a study guide for the test.
4. Studying with other students for the test.
5. Thinking about the test on the way to class.
6. Walking into the classroom on test day.
7. Receiving the test from the teacher.
8. Reading the first question on the test.
9. Looking at your watch during the test.
10. Not knowing the answer to a test question.

Your list should consist of no fewer than 10 items and no more than 25. The degree of the anxiety will determine the number of scenes on the hierarchy with the scene provoking the least anxiety being number one, the next least anxiety-producing scene being number two, etc.

Also included in the development of the list is the identification of one scene which is associated with complete relaxation, and this should be numbered zero. This scene is called the control scene. The control scene should be unrelated to the anxiety-producing situation and thoughts of the control scene should result in total comfort and relaxation. For the student taking the examination, perhaps lying on the beach on a warm day with the sun shining and gentle waves rolling onto the shore is a control scene which produces total relaxation and comfort.

Now that you have mastered relaxation and constructed your list, it is time to put the two together during the third stage of systematic desensitization. While you are fully relaxed, imagine the first scene on your list. It is important to imagine a very clear, vivid, and detailed scene. If this scene is visualized without experiencing anxiety, imagine the second scene on your list. This procedure is continued until each scene on the list can be visualized without anxiety. If at any time you experience anxiety, stop the visualization of that scene and imagine the control scene with an anxiety rating of zero. When you are totally relaxed once again, return to the scene prior to the one that made you anxious. Visualize this scene once again and continue up the scale as before.

Using our previous list, let's see how stage three might work for you if you are anxious about taking tests. We will assume that you have mastered progressive relaxation, as described previously, and have constructed the list of scenes above. Now you find a place to relax and imagine the first scene on the list - seeing the test date on the course description. You might see yourself sitting in a classroom with other students. Imagine how they are dressed, how the desk feels, how the room is arranged, etc., in an attempt to create as vivid an image as possible. Then imagine the teacher's handing out a paper which lists all the course requirements. While remaining completely relaxed, imagine seeing the date of the first test. Picturing this scene does not produce anxiety so you proceed to the next scene. In this scene, imagine yourself in the same classroom with the teacher standing at a lectern in the front of the room. Then try to imagine how the instructor might be dressed, how he might talk, walk, and what type of person he is. Now imagine the teacher's announcing that the test will be next Wednesday. As you imagine this scene, you are aware of anxiety, and so you quickly switch to the control scene and imagine lying on the beach with the sun shining and gentle waves rolling in. After a few moments of this visualization, you are again relaxed. As you return to the list, you go back to the previous scene - imagine seeing the first test date on the course description and visualize that scene while completely relaxed. Then return to the scene of the teacher's announcing the first test date. At this point, the anxiety should be lessened. If you are still experiencing anxiety, perhaps you need to reconsider the list. You might want to add another intermediate step. For example, you might insert a scene between one and two in which you are entering the classroom and overhear the teacher's discussing the test date with another student. The first three steps of the new hierarchy would change to:

1. Seeing the test date on the course description.
2. Hearing the teacher's discussing the test with another student.
3. Having the teacher announce the first test.

It is helpful to remember that this is your list and you can arrange it any way that is most useful to you. It is also helpful to remember that you might need additional help with this exercise if you have difficulty imagining the scenes or staying relaxed. If you experience difficulty, you might consider consulting the counseling center on your campus.

This technique of systematic desensitization teaches you to remain relaxed in situations which previously produced anxiety. Because you are more relaxed in these situations, stress is reduced. And, you are also more relaxed when anticipating these situations.

Time Management

Another important coping skill for returning students or anyone who is making a major life change is learning to manage time. As a returning student, the allocation of time is a critical issue because you are frequently involved in multiple roles such as spouse, parent, employee, etc. - and now you are adding another one as a student! The more roles you attempt, the greater the chance of depleting the supply of time and energy you have and the more likely there will be conflicts between some of the demands of these roles. For example, in your role as wife perhaps you have always cooked dinner, and now as a student, you find you have a class that meets during that time. These conflicts can increase stress.

To aid in the prevention of additional stress, time management is a very important consideration. The steps that follow should assist you in learning to manage your day more efficiently.

1. Inventory your time by recording how you utilize your time during the day. Include your working hours, class time, recreational time, preparation of meals, time spent car-pooling children, and time spent waiting in doctor's or dentist's offices. After a week of recording your time, you will begin to see patterns emerge. These patterns will help you in setting priorities.

2. Prepare a weekly time schedule based on your recorded inventory. Try to set aside a time to study each day rather than studying in long "cram" sessions. If you find that you have "dead" time during the day when you are waiting for someone or something, think of ways to utilize the time. You might prepare note cards to study during these times or take a textbook with you to read as you are waiting. If you find it too distracting to read in these situations, then take a "fun" reading book or activity and use this as recreational time. I know one student who carried postcards with her all the time, and whenever she had to wait in line, she wrote notes to family and friends.

Working from a written schedule will help you to manage time more efficiently. In Appendix B is an example of a scheduling chart that might be helpful in preparing your weekly time schedule.

3. Make daily "to do" lists. Prioritize your list by labeling the most important task for the day as #1. If your #1 seems too overwhelming and you have difficulty crossing that item off your list, break it into smaller segments. For example, if item #1 is "get ready to start school," that's probably too large a task. You could break item #1 down into several steps, such as:

#1. See advisor.
#2. Go to registrar's office to have classes scheduled.
#3. Visit bursar's office to pay fees.
#4. Visit bookstore to buy books.
#5. Locate classrooms on campus.

Prioritized "to do" lists can also help you to prepare for tests or other school projects. List exactly what steps will help you to accomplish the task and then set aside the time to do it. There is one caution, however. Do not become a slave to your lists! I know one student who used the lists to "punish" herself. If she didn't finish everything on her list every day, she used this as evidence that she was disorganized, lazy, etc. And this added stress to her life, rather than reducing it. It is important to be flexible, to realize that some days you will accomplish more than others, and to accept that Murphy's Law still applies sometimes.

If you don't manage to complete everything on your list for one day, take the unfinished items and put them on the next day's list. In this way, all the things that need to be done will eventually be accomplished. And if there is some task that keeps getting moved from one day to the next, consider the possibility that maybe it is something that is not really that important or maybe someone else could do it.

4. Delegate chores at home and/or work. By the assignment of chores, others may become more helpful and the load will be lessened. Help may come from a spouse, child, co-worker, or friend. For example, have a problem-solving session (as described later in this chapter) with your family or co-workers to distribute the workload more equitably. Include your children in the daily chores by having them empty the dishwasher or start dinner. Delegating chores, no matter how small, can create additional uncommitted time for you to spend on tasks that have a higher priority. It can also help prevent added stress and the depletion of energy.

Through logical planning, efficient organizing, prioritizing tasks, and delegating work, you will be using your time wisely. You will experience the gratification of intermediate accomplishments while reaching long-term goals with a minimum of stress.

Cognitive Coping Skills

Cognitive coping skills consist of techniques which help us change our thought patterns and therefore influence our feelings and ultimately our behavior. But they must be learned and practiced until they become almost automatic, and that requires an investment of time and energy. Another caution about these techniques is that they are most effective when used **prior to** the situations which are anxiety and fear arousing. Once you are in the grip of a panic attack, it is too late to learn them. The physiological effects of the adrenaline pumping through your system override attempts to think rationally and calmly. So, I encourage you to put forth the time and effort to learn these techniques before you actually need them.

Cognitive events are conscious thoughts that occur which can be readily retrieved when requested. When someone asks you "what are you thinking," he or she is asking you to share the cognitive event which is occurring in your head. These cognitive events have also been called automatic thoughts (Beck, 1976) and internal dialogue (Meichenbaum, 1977). Automatic thoughts or internal dialogue typically occur in specific situations, such as when we are learning a new skill, when we have to make choices and judgments, and when we experience or anticipate an intense emotional experience. Many times these cognitive events are so automatic that it might take us a moment or two to think of a time when they occurred. Try to remember the last time you were in a highly charged emotional situation. Perhaps one of your children was injured or you received news of a loved one's death. Recreate the situation in your mind and remember what you were saying to yourself. Most of us give ourselves instructions or guidance in these situations. And, such cognitive events do not have to be talking - they can be mental images or symbolic pictures. Perhaps you repeated to yourself to remain calm, to telephone someone, or otherwise instructed yourself. In the case of the injured child, you might have been instructing yourself to get the phone book and call the doctor or find the newspaper and locate the emergency room of the day. Each of these cognitive events helped you to cope with the situation and was instrumental in producing behaviors which led to a resolution of the situation as well as a reduction in the anxiety.

Unfortunately some of the automatic thoughts you have are not helpful in resolving situations which are problematic. In fact, they can interfere with a successful resolution. These are the automatic thoughts which you want to change. The first step in changing them is to become aware of them.

In order to become aware of these cognitive events, you have to practice keeping track of what you are thinking. I suggest that at least twice a day, stop what you are doing and take a moment to ask yourself "What am I thinking?" Try to "catch your thoughts." Then spend a few minutes trying to recall an event which was emotionally arousing and try to remember what you were thinking. Don't wear yourself out trying to do this, just make yourself aware of your thoughts. Perhaps you could think about making the decision to return to school and be aware of all the things you are thinking and feeling. Make a note of these thoughts. Are they mostly positive or negative? Do they produce anxiety, tension, or fear in you? Or you could think about the first day at school and imagine how you are going to feel and what you will be thinking to yourself. Are you afraid of not being able to find the right rooms or being older than the typical college student? Or you could think about making a class presentation. What are the things you are saying to yourself as you imagine being in these situations? Are they positive statements which are likely to help you cope with the situation or negative statements which are likely to intensify what you are feeling and interfere with your ability to function?

Once you have determined the typical style of your cognitive events in these potentially fear-arousing and stressful situations, you are ready to try to change them. Meichenbaum (1977) suggests the following techniques to inoculate yourself against stressful situations:

1. Assess the reality of the situation and control negative thoughts.
2. Use and possibly relabel the anxiety you are experiencing.
3. Perform the task while attempting to control the anxiety you feel.
4. Reinforce yourself for coping.

Let's take one situation and see how we might apply each of these steps to that situation. You are about to take your first test in school. You sit down to study and are suddenly aware of negative thoughts. First, you need to assess the reality of the situation. Perhaps you are thinking, "If I fail this test, I might as well drop out of school. It will prove that I'm just too old to do this." The reality of the situation (as any college student can tell you) is that a college career is not based on any single test. Even if you were to fail this one, it does not mean you can't do the work. It might mean that you need to do more studying, to learn more effective study skills, or to take a lower level course first. But, failing one test doesn't **prove** anything.

Next, use and relabel the anxiety you are feeling. Tell yourself that everyone gets nervous before an examination. Those who don't get nervous typically aren't motivated to study and do well. So feeling nervous (not panicked) is good and should help you to feel motivated to study. Tell yourself that a little anxiety will actually improve your performance (which is true!). Also **use** this anxiety. Go to the room where you will take the test at a time when it is unoccupied. Sit down and imagine the instructor's passing out the test. Make mental coping statements to yourself such as "I am relaxed. I have studied this material, and I will do well on this test." Repeat this procedure until you feel comfortable in the room.

Third, go and take the test. Even though you may still be anxious, recognize that this is natural and all the students are feeling anxious, make yourself do it. Remember to breathe deeply when you feel overwhelmed and to make calming statements to yourself. If it is a timed test and you tend to get overly concerned about finishing, then don't wear a watch. Also, if you tend to worry about how many questions are left, start at the end of the test and work backwards. If you don't know strategies for taking tests, read the introductory material in any of the preparation books for standardized tests such as the Scholastic Aptitude Test (SAT). **And**, use the relaxation procedures outlined in this chapter.

Fourth, mentally reward yourself for coping with the situation by making positive self-statements such as, "I did it," "I am pleased with my progress in coping," or "I finished it - good for me!"

If you happen to be returning to school after a particularly stressful life event, such as divorce or the last child's leaving home, you may have some leftover negative emotions and thoughts which can interfere with success. In particular, if these events have had a negative impact on your self-image, you may invest a lot of emotional energy in your success in school, which may be converted into a measure of your self-esteem. For example, you may feel that you are really a rotten person who can't do anything right if you don't make all A's. As much as possible, even if it means getting professional help, try to restructure these expectations. Through positive self-talk, remind yourself of all the things you do well, the things you have done and continue to do in which you can take pride. Remember that grades are not a measure of the person that you are and YOU ARE NOT YOUR GRADES. It may take some extra work to keep reminding yourself of this, but it is well worth the effort.

Many returning students with whom I work have particular problems in mathematics courses for various reasons. They are usually surprised when I tell them all you really need to graduate is a "D." Often they protest loudly that a D is just not good enough. My response is, "Why isn't a D good enough?" Usually their answers indicate that for some reason they believe they have to be "better" than a D and that it would be a serious injury to their self-esteem if they didn't make a "good" grade. Albert Ellis calls these irrational cognitions, and you need to confront them head-on. The reality of the situation is that, unless they have a very low grade point average, a D is good enough for them to graduate and it has nothing to do with the kind of person that they are. Students are always surprised when I tell them that I will not think any less of them if they make a D in mathematics. I will still think they are highly motivated, intelligent students who just happen to have some difficulty in mathematic courses. Not everyone can be perfect, or even good, in all academic areas. And it is really not a reflection on them if they don't perform at high levels in all academic areas. As long as they pass the required courses, maintain an average grade point average, and accumulate the required number of hours, they will graduate. With this in mind, try to reduce some of the additional stress caused by expecting to be perfect in all academic areas.

Another irrational cognition that may be problematic for returning students is that they have to do everything they used to do and still make all A's. College is very demanding of your time, and it is going to require some adjustments in your schedule. If you have a spouse and/or children who are accustomed to certain services that you perform, there may have to be adjustments in your schedule to accommodate these changes. Naturally you can expect some resistance to these changes. Your significant others may be very supportive of your decision to return to school because they haven't realized how many changes there will be. And later, when it becomes obvious how many changes are necessary, they are likely to resist. The best strategy is to try to anticipate the necessary changes prior to enrollment and be aware of what your needs are likely to be. Many schools conduct orientation programs specifically for returning students. Attend if at all possible. This should give you the information you need to assess the changes in lifestyle that will be required as well as the information required to anticipate your needs. When you have identified these needs, try to compromise with your significant others as much as possible with a very realistic problem-solving approach. Every person has needs to be met. It is a matter of deciding how best to meet as many needs of the parties concerned as possible, with the clear understanding that it may be impossible to meet **all** of everyone's needs. A non-emotional discussion and problem-solving session can go a long way in getting the full cooperation of your family.

Problem-Solving Strategies

D'Zurilla and Goldfried (1971) suggest a problem-solving strategy that may be useful not only in negotiating with your significant others but also for other problems that might arise. Basically it consists of the following five steps.

First, recognize the problem. This may seem almost comical in its simplicity, but in fact it may be the most difficult. Anyone who has tried to convince someone they have a problem, such as alcohol or drug abuse or procrastination, usually meets with resistance. We all seem reluctant to admit to a problem. Even if we do admit it, we often stop there as if that were all we needed to do. In the case or procrastination, for example, you might admit to the problem as an explanation and never take the next step to solve the problem. Or, we admit that we are overweight and never take the steps to reduce. It is perfectly acceptable to have a problem and choose not to work on it - but the problem should not then become an excuse for taking no action. In recognizing the problem, we also need to admit that there is a good possibility that we can solve the problem if we act systematically and thoughtfully, not impulsively.

Second, define the problem. As thoroughly as possible, specify the history of the problem and be specific about the exact problem. For example, many students might say the problem is that their grades are not good enough when the actual problem may be a lack of scheduled study time or study skills.

Generation of alternatives is the third step in the process. At this stage, you are simply trying to generate as many alternatives as possible. Do not concern yourself with the plausibility of these solutions. Be as creative, innovative, and even as silly as you can. Do not judge these alternatives at this time. If possible, consult with other people who may have had a similar problem and ask how they solved it. Or enlist the aid of friends in generating alternatives.

Fourth, make a decision. In this step, you want to examine each of the alternatives carefully and try to evaluate the outcome of the implementation of each of them. Then select the alternative that seems to provide the optimum solution and put it into effect.

Fifth, monitor the effectiveness of the plan. Does it solve the problem? If not, try another of the alternatives that were generated in the fourth step. With each new attempt, continue to check to see if the solution worked. Don't be discouraged if the first solution does not work, sometimes they don't. If you have tried several alternatives that have not worked, you might reconsider the problem definition. Sometimes the solution isn't working because we haven't correctly identified the problem.

Let's take an example and see how the steps might work with a problem in a math course. You have now taken two quizzes in the course and have grades of 80 and 65. You are concerned because you do not want to make a low grade in this course. You have been doing all the assigned homework and attending every class, but you are beginning to wonder if you understand the material as well as you think you do. This problem started with a particular set of information which was presented in a class one week ago. The instructor has informed you that your lack of understanding of that information is going to seriously affect your performance the rest of the quarter. What to do?

You could withdraw from the course and take it later. You could hire a tutor to help you catch up. You could do nothing and try to struggle through. You could find another student who made a better grade on the second test to help you with the material. These are just some of the possible alternatives you might consider. Now, what are the likely implications and probabilities associated with each of these alternatives? Perhaps if you withdraw from the course, it will delay graduation or prevent you from taking the next course in a sequence when it is offered. If you hire a tutor, it would require additional financial resources and an additional commitment of time to meet with the tutor. Trying to struggle through without any help might result in success or more likely in frustration, stress, and failure. Finding another student to help you might work if you are the type of person who meets people easily and doesn't mind asking for assistance from others. Each person's situation is different, and only you can ultimately determine which of these possible alternatives best fits into your life scheme. But once you have determined which alternative is best for you, then proceed to put that solution into effect. After the next test, evaluate the success of your solution based on your understanding of the material and your grade. If the solution you selected is not working, then try the next most likely solution.

Problem-solving is a skill that can be learned, and it improves with practice. It can be used in a variety of ways and with a variety of problems. The advantage of a specific technique for problem solving is that it provides a general framework that is easily utilized in many different situations.

All of the coping strategies presented in this chapter are fairly easy to implement in your life and lead to reduced stress, frustration, and anxiety. They do require some practice, however, and some motivation to change. Even if you are not particularly motivated right now, keep the ideas in mind so you can use them later if you need them.

References

Beck, A. T. (1976) Cognitive Therapy and the Emotional Disorders. New York: International Universities Press.

Borkovec, Thomas and Berstein, Douglas (1975). Progressive Relaxation Training. Champaign, ILL.: Research Press.

D'Zurilla, T. J., & Goldfried, M. R. (1971). Problem Solving and Behavior Modification. Journal of Abnormal Psychology, 78, 107-126.

Jacobson, Edmund (1938). Progressive Relaxation. Chicago: University of Chicago Press.

Meichenbaum, D. (1977) Cognitive Behavior Modification: An Integrative Approach. New York: Plenum.

Ornish, Dean. (1982) Stress, Diet and Your Heart. New York: Holt, Rinehart and Winston.

Selye, Hans (1976) The Stress of Life (2nd ed.) New York: McGraw-Hill.

Wolpe, Joseph (1958) Psychotherapy by Reciprocal Inhibition. Stanford: Stanford Press.

PART IV

Administrative and Instructional Adjustments

Administrative and faculty awareness that returning students are unique in their needs and deserve special programs, adjusted schedules, and flexible curriculums is the subject of this part. Grades are not to be sent to parents nor is parental approval needed for activities. Older students need a curriculum and schedule that reflect institutional respect for their job and family life. While Chapter 9 speaks to the administrator, Chapter 10 alerts the classroom instructor of differences in these students. Instructors should provide mature students the opportunity to show what they are capable of accomplishing and to further their journey toward a degree and better life.

The initial narrative is written by an instructor who relates his personal experience of discovering students in his class who are both older and perhaps wiser than he.

BILL'S STORY

Walking into the classroom, placing written notes on the table, adjusting the podium, and making eye contact with willing students are routine for the first day of class. But when it's the very first college class you've ever taught, routine is hardly the word to describe it -- especially when the dean had only moments before told you what you would teach, handed you two books, and headed you in the direction of room 115. I had just finished teaching all day in a maximum security prison for men so I feebly attempted to reassure myself that this class couldn't be too tough.

Since I had no time to look over the book, my only option was to ad lib about the course in general. I told the students how many exams to expect as well as the type questions I intended to use. I went on to explain why developmental psychology is important, its contributions to mankind, etc. Yes, I was bluffing while assuring myself I would definitely know a lot more at the next class meeting.

As I began a closer look at the students, recognizing them as individuals, I noticed several older men and one middle aged woman. I soon discovered that one of the men was a former military pilot, one man was a retired police officer, and the lady was a single parent with children. She had returned to school to improve her marketability and the family's financial prospects. The ex-military man was supportive: he nodded frequently as if to reassure me everything was fine; the retired gentleman appeared to be just coasting along, hearing only what he wanted to absorb, but the lady was in a full learning mode -- reaching for every word I said as if there would be a test any minute.

During my initial classes, I was uneasy thinking that some of these people, experts in their fields, would expect "expertness" from me. They had paid their money, bought books, and were giving me their time, a part of their life. I felt compelled to be that expert with all the answers. This worried me as I realized it would take much more than a few days of review for me to become an "expert" developmental psychology instructor.

Since that first class, now some 20 later, I remember those feelings. I've also heard other instructors, especially younger ones, express concern about students in their classes who were old enough to be their parents or grandparents.

I quickly discovered that these mature students contribute much to the stability and motivation of the entire class. The younger students seem to realize that they are now in the real world, a world of military people, teachers, professionals, and retirees. The unifying thread (which is frequently a shock to an 18 or 19 year old) is that all students are in the class for the same reason -- to learn. They want and need the information a college provides in order to make their lives more complete and fulfilling. Discussing theories and studies with the policeman or grandmother in the next seat seems to give education and learning a different perspective from what it was in high school.

Hired as an instructor, I set out to face the challenge of teaching one or two classes in higher education. I immediately got hooked on the contagious enthusiasm of both the younger and older students. They invested their time and hard work while asking for nothing in return but fairness. But they deserve much more. They need and deserve a large share of my time, my sincere encouragement, my interest in answering their questions, my efforts to remain current on the issues in their areas of study, and my caring about what happens to them. With the goals of fulfilling these needs for my students, teaching is a lot easier and even more rewarding. I welcome the challenge of making students feel worthy although they may have stumbled in math and received a "C," or helping them realize there is no shame in not knowing how to complete a graph or understanding what "recidivism" means. I have found that with a little reassurance and encouragement even the most insecure students can become graduates with confidence and pride -- eager to move further in their lives.   As a teacher, I can offer each student a word of encouragement and a helping hand. It's amazing -- as I attempt to encourage and motivate my students, I find they do the same for me.   I find myself able to accomplish more as a result of witnessing students converting my encouraging "you can" into a positive "I can" and then do the seemingly impossible!

Chapter 9

TRANSFORMING ADMINISTRATIVE PHILOSOPHY INTO INVOLVEMENT

Linda R. Jenkins

Busy student affairs administrators are always looking for tried and true ideas which can be easily adapted to fit their campus. Seldom does a successful program at one institution transfer to another campus without some alterations. This chapter is not meant to tell you exactly what to do for returning students on your campus but rather is intended to stimulate your own thinking about your students.

Improving Educational Environments for Adults by Nancy K. Schlossberg, Ann Q. Lynch, and Arthur W. Chickering (1989) is perhaps the single most useful resource I have found in almost 10 years of working with returning students. It gives excellent background information as well as practical suggestions for helping adult students as they "move in" to the higher education system, "move through" the institution in search of academic and personal fulfillment, and "move on" from higher education to new roles in life.

The authors suggest that student affairs administrators view themselves as educators rather than merely service providers. It is true that our backgrounds as administrators vary. Some of us are more interested in the business-like aspects of managing programs while others prefer more of the personal contact with students through counseling and workshop situations. Whatever our orientation or place in the organizational chart, we, as student affairs professionals, are indeed part of the total educational program of the institution. We must keep that perspective as we work to understand and develop programs for our adult learners and all our students.

Research by Aslanian and Brickell (1980) indicates that most adults who enter college do so as the result of some change in their life. These life transitions are most often triggered by family changes for women who return to school. For men, the transition is most often triggered by career changes. As student affairs educators, we must keep these "triggers" in mind as we attempt to recruit and retain adult students.

Cross (1981) discusses research on barriers to adult learning. This research includes learning in many settings, including higher education. She classifies obstacles to learning into three categories: situational, institutional, and dispositional. A situational barrier is related to one's situation in life at a certain time. Lack of funds, transportation, or child care are all examples of situational barriers. Institutional barriers include those practices and procedures of the institution which discourage adults. These may include inconvenient class scheduling and too much red tape in getting enrolled. Dispositional barriers are more personal and related to attitudes and self-perceptions the prospective student has about themself. These barriers involve personal fears about being too old to learn or lack of energy.

We must analyze the barriers in our own institutions. We must also recognize that nontraditional students are quickly becoming today's traditional students. Old ways of thinking and responding to student needs have to be adjusted. If universities are to maintain the enrollments they have grown to expect, they must do more than allow adults to take classes--they must encourage them to attend. Administrators who recognize the value of a diverse student population must also face the frustration of developing programs and services to meet the diverse needs of all students.

Schlossberg, Lynch, and Chickering (1989) emphasize that institutions need to act as though each student matters. Those in leadership positions in student affairs and throughout the institution should make it clear to everyone that students do matter. As administrators, it may be necessary to spend more time educating staff about the institution's mission and how returning students fit into that mission. Those not in leadership positions should be educated to recognize the importance of every contact with students. Their helpfulness may make the difference for a student who would otherwise give up when a problem is encountered. The stories of returning students who encounter a disgruntled clerk in the admissions office (or financial aid or elsewhere) and decide not to enroll are all too familiar. Fortunately, the reverse is also true. Many times a helpful clerk or secretary makes such a favorable impression on a returning student that the student assumes all encounters at the institution will be so positive.

How do we communicate to adult students that they do, in fact, matter to the institution? One obvious way is to picture adults in campus publications. Most schools have one or more brochures they use in student recruitment. Even when there is a special brochure for returning students, it is important that photographs in all publications show the diversity of the student body. This communicates to prospective students and to the community that the institution recognizes the value of each segment of the student population. It also lets older students know that they will not be alone on campus.

Another practical suggestion for communicating with adults thinking about a return to college is to look critically at all the forms, letters, and brochures sent to potential students. Does the language refer to the traditional 18 year old still dependent on his or her parents? Is the information written in terms that can be easily interpreted without the help of a high school counselor or someone familiar with higher education terminology?

Every student affairs educator should be a listener. We should listen to students and listen to staff who listen to students. Where do you hear the most complaints? Is parking a problem?

Can students eat in the cafeteria if they have special dietary needs? Are administrative and academic offices open during lunch and after 5 p.m.? Is the bookstore open at night? Is the library open on Saturday morning? Are academic advisors available for night students? Listening lets students know they matter. Frequently the only thing you need to do is let students know you will listen. They may not expect anyone to "do" anything, but they do expect someone to listen to them.

One of the most exciting and, at the same time, the most challenging aspects of working with college students of all ages is that nothing stays the same. Students' needs change. We have to be flexible. Rather than trying to fit the students into our traditional mold, we have to adapt to their needs. For returning students, this means that one year we may have a very structured support organization for returning students. Another year may bring entirely new concerns and we need do nothing more than keep a coffee pot going and serve as a resource center.

William Giczkowski wrote in "Colleges must learn to cope with market-oriented adult students" (The Chronicle of Higher Education, 1990) that "adult re-entry students tend to see themselves as consumers and frequently approach academic administrators with questions that sound suspiciously like demands for customer service." Returning students are busy: their time is important. They are also used to our consumer-oriented society where the customer expects services available after working hours and provided by professional, courteous staff who give them individual attention. Colleges cannot, and should not be expected to, adjust every procedure to suit each student's demands, but they certainly can be reasonable. If a prospective student makes a quick trip to campus during lunch to get an admissions package, he or she should also be able to get a financial aid brochure and catalog without having to search for another parking space across campus.

It is helpful to periodically evaluate every aspect of the system for meeting the educational needs of students. Walk through the system yourself, completing each step from the student's point of view. It may not be necessary to change the way a procedure is done; however, it may be very important that staff who have direct student contact know why a certain procedure is necessary. Students and staff who understand the logic behind a requirement or procedure are more involved in the educational process and can be very helpful in explaining procedures to others. Be prepared, however, because adult students will tell you when a procedure appears unnecessary, and many times they are right!

If possible, the institution should appoint a particular person or designate an office to respond to the needs of returning students. This is especially important for entering students and prospective students who have questions that may cross departmental lines. This resource person should know about people and procedures in every department so busy students have to make fewer trips around campus. Sometimes returning students need as much help articulating their questions as they do in getting their questions answered. Personnel trained in working with returning students generally know when students need more information.

Many returning students have told me that they would like to have a specific place on campus reserved for them. They like the idea of being able to meet other returning students and having some social interaction with students who share their interests and needs. Some colleges designate a room or lounge just for returning students. Of course, it is possible for students to create an unofficial gathering place by always congregating in the same area of the student lounge.

Identify your students' concerns. This may be done by purchasing or developing an extensive assessment program or by informally talking to your students. You may also get valuable information from a returning student advisory committee. "Assessment" is the buzz word for the '90s in higher education. If the results from your assessment of students' needs lead to an improved educational environment for your students, it will indeed be worthwhile.

Some colleges have developed comprehensive returning student centers which offer everything from specialized orientation for entering students to job placement for returning student graduates. Many schools offer special workshops designed for returning students through departments already established on campus. For example, a counseling center designed to assist all students may offer a workshop for single parents or a program on time management. An established learning center may adapt their programs offered to traditional students and create a special program for returning students on test anxiety or on how to take multiple choice exams.

Some student programming committees are beginning to offer lectures and entertainment events geared toward the interests of older students. Rather than always depending on others to meet their co-curricular needs, adult students should be encouraged to become active participants on planning committees of the programming board or student government. Campus child care may become an issue when returning students become active in student government. The student newspaper may report on free family entertainment and list advertisements for co-op child care arrangements when adult students become involved on the staff of the campus paper. Some schools have even developed newsletters devoted entirely to the interests of older students.

Colleges have responded to the influx of returning students in many ways. Those that saw the adult learner only as a way to fill empty classrooms without adjusting schedules, services, or attitudes will learn, if they have not already, that adult students won't continue to enroll if their needs are ignored. They will find other ways to meet their needs for education. Colleges that have recognized the wealth of knowledge and experience brought to campus by adult students and have encouraged their participation have gained, not only in the number of adult students attending their classes, but also in the richness added to classroom discussion and the campus community.

Extending a hand to returning students is beneficial to the college as well as to the student. When students perceive that the institution cares and supports them, they are not only more likely to continue pursuing their own educational goals at the college, they will serve as its best recruiters for other returning students.

References

Aslania, Carol B. & Brickell, Henry M. (1980). <u>Americans in Transition: Life Changes as Reasons for Adult Learning.</u> Princeton: College Board.

Cross, Patricia K. (1981) <u>Adults as Learners.</u> San Francisco: Jossey-Bass.

Giczkowski, William (1990). Colleges must learn to cope with market-oriented adult students. <u>Chronicle of Higher Education, 36,</u> April 4th.

Schlossberg, Nancy K., Lynch, Ann Q., & Chickering, Arthur W. (1989). <u>Improving Higher Education Environments for Adults</u>. San Francisco: Jossey-Bass.

Chapter 10

ADJUSTING TO A DIFFERENT GENERATION

Del Witherspoon

In a mobile society with overnight changes in technology, new skills and information must be sought by some and taught by others. This chapter is directed to those teaching adult students which today includes nearly everyone teaching in a college, university, or technical classroom.

Understanding how adult students differ from more traditional students can be intriguing as well as beneficial to educators. We can no longer accept the concept that maturation progresses through a predictable smooth pattern as projected by the developmental theories formulated earlier in this century. The current value of these sequential developmental theories is questionable. Erikson's theory of development (1950) requires the resolution of certain conflicting components before an individual reaches a later stage. Today it appears that some stages are by-passed without resolution. Perhaps stages of development or phases tied to a chronological linear process must be viewed in respect to events in specific areas of life as today, in American society, work, family, friends, and community are more segmented or independent. Even variables such as gender become a less important consideration. It may be that many adults who return to school are temporarily stepping out of the mainstream of society on which sequential theories were designed. Therefore, the predictors discussed by Sheehy (1976) and Gould (1978) are not applicable to the adults found on today's college campuses.

Though much has been written relative to adult education, most of it addresses vocational training, GED preparation, or continuing education courses. The focus in this book is on adult learning as it relates to higher education in regular college courses. This chapter provides a short review of man's interest in "learning" and discusses three factors inherent to learning on the college campus: the recipient, in this case the returning student; the instructor or professor; and the material, its format, and how it's presented.

Man's Interest in Learning

I suspect man has pondered his ability to acquire, remember, and utilize information since he began walking the earth; however, his intellectual efforts at theorizing about learning and educational philosophy did not begin to mature until the latter part of the nineteenth century. Learning is generally defined as "an enduring change in the neural mechanisms of behavior that results from experience with environmental events" (Domjan and Burkhard, 1986). Major influences on learning theory include: the pragmatism of Dewey, the connectionism of Thorndike, the classical conditioning of Pavlov; the operant conditioning of Skinner; the contiguity of Guthrie; the cognitive maps of Tolman; the drive reduction of Hull; the mathematical model of Spence; the perceptual whole of Gestalt; the cognitive development of Piaget; the modeling of Bandura; the learning sets of Harlow; the hierarchical processes of Gagne; and the field theory of Lewin.

The specific interest in adult learning was accelerated by two early books: E. C. Lindeman's The Meaning of Adult Education in 1926 and Thorndike's Adult Learning in 1928.

As teachers, we are interested in transforming the theories of learning into theories or principles of teaching. Contributors in this effort include: Gage, Hilgard, Gagne, Bloom, and Tough. Focusing more directly on adult education, Malcolm Knowles (1973) writes of the "andragoical" theory of adult learning as opposed to "pedagogy." He borrowed the term from theorists in Europe to emphasize the difference between how self-directed adults should be taught as compared to how youth should be taught. Because too often we attempt to teach adults by the methods established for teaching youth, he refers to our current educational process as being a "progressively regressive educational system."

The Recipient

As recipients of educational materials, returning students may be quite different from younger, traditional students. Besides many varied experiences and different motivations for learning, adult students are also undergoing different mental and physical changes. First we will look at the unique motivations and influences from their prior experiences and life roles before turning to some of the basic maturational changes.

The returning students sitting in your class are most likely all involved in self-examinations of their lives; however, the event that triggered this reexamination is probably different for each one. As a result of the triggering event, which might involve retirement, disability, children growing up, a lay-off, divorce, or death, they are exploring new lifestyles. Returning to college is a major lifestyle change for adults.

In Chapter 4, Susan Dudley discusses the multiple roles in which adults are now involved. Becoming a student adds yet another role. Perhaps interfacing adult development with participation in multiple roles is helpful in understanding adults who return to college. Such an approach has been studied by Hughes, Graham, and Galbraith (1986). More recently Hughes an Graham (1990) found a surprisingly large degree of diversity in individual development when comparing different roles, such as those involving relationships with self, work, family, and others. They suggest that in each of these areas adults progress through four phases: initiation, which is a period of getting involved; adaptation, which brings new adjustments; reassessment, which is a time for examination; and reconciliation, a time for reflection. Their findings were interesting in that adults, involved in many different roles, had progressed to different stages within each role. They stated, "Adults who engage in the life role of work and do not engage in the family life role until they are well-established in their careers would be well advanced in the work-life role, but inexperienced in the tasks, behaviors, and expectations of family roles they had not assumed."

Just because students appear mature in many respects doesn't mean they are adept at learning; however, their advanced basic life skills allow them to adjust quickly. The mature students in your class may still be in the initiation phase or just into the adaptation phase in some life-roles. That first quarter or semester can prove enlightening or devastating to their educational efforts and goals.

Classrooms today contain a diverse student population seeking to learn but having different reasons and motivations for learning. These older students are different from those on the GI Bill who registered for classes immediately after World War II or the more recent conflicts. The majority of GI students were males in their 20s who were seeking marketable skills. Over half of today's adult students are also seeking economic alternatives, yet many are in school to meet the challenge of completing a life-long educational goal or for self-improvement. There is a small group who are only seeking mental stimulation as they search within themselves for meaning in their life. The needs of today's older students are quite different. Some of these adults are satisfied with non-credited courses; however, some feel comfortable in the classroom and appreciate the social contacts, the challenge, and the pressures of deadlines and exams for credited courses.

Students over 40 have unique expectations from their educational pursuits. They view their college experience from a different perspective and from a different social reality. They intend to use what they learn differently from younger students. Many seek mental stimulation and/or wisdom while not being so concerned with economic survival. During their late 40s, many are able to shift attention from raising a family, from being productive, from being a pawn in society to being a free, critical observer, a doer seeking to understand the scope and nature of the society in which they live.

At mid-life, different needs develop, values are reassessed, emotions are different, intentions and ambitions vary. The ability to integrate knowledge and the intuition for growth have matured through years of experience and are quite prevalent around mid-age.   Adult learners over 40 appear to be independent, responsible, and very self-directed. They accept ambiguities more easily than traditional students. Motivation comes from within rather than from an economic need. Their perspectives of the world have changed.   Accordingly, methods for instructing students over 40 must change.

While education for mature students must be geared to their mid-life developmental stage, education for the young adult continues to focus on helping the learner to compete and be accepted and successful within the context of society.   Their motivation is, therefore, geared to material gain. Young students are taught using productive content that is analytical, unambiguous, technical, and practical, reflecting a stable society. This is not what older students respond to.   According to McWhinney (1990), learning for older adults needs to be integrative,   self-reflective,   concerned   with   validity   and authenticity, synthetic, critical, and dialectical.

Physical as well as mental changes are unique to students who have reached mid-age.   Because the structure of the eye continues to change throughout life, reduced visual perception becomes a problem as people reach their 40s. As the lens of the eye become less elastic, farsightedness or presbyopia develops. Color differentiation maybe another obstacle to older students. Botwinick (1978) reported that older students become increasingly confused between the colors blue and green. Loss of visual acuity suggests materials should be presented with adequate size and space to minimize interference. Due to decreased ability to adapt quickly to changes in lighting, some illumination should be available during slides and films for safety purposes.

Hearing can be another challenge for older adults. Human hearing peaks during the teens and then declines. There is a marked decrease in the ability to hear higher frequencies. The transmission of neural impulses from the receptors and within the perceptual areas of the brain become less efficient. Due to these discrepancies in hearing and processing, surrounding sounds interfere and are more of a distraction for older students. Traffic noises, noises in the hallway, or whispering in the classroom are major problems for returning students. Instructors can take steps to ensure that oral presentations are delivered in a manner that all students can comfortably hear.

Although mental characteristics are changing for older students, they should not necessarily be viewed as a handicap. Being aware of how age affects certain functions can be advantageous to both the teacher and the student. Adults search their accumulation of knowledge for techniques to find the best solution to existing problems. They tend to rely on reproductive thinking or what has worked in the past rather than creating and implementing new techniques. They are, therefore, inclined to use non-productive strategies and to repeat these strategies, even when they don't work. When a novel problem is confronted and none of the solutions accumulated over the years work, their performance may be less efficient than younger students (Birren, 1964). Older students should be encouraged to be creative in their thinking processes and to dare to initiate untried solutions to novel problems.

As for intelligence, both longitudinal and cross-sectional studies indicate that IQ remains stable up to the age of 50. Roberts (1968), however, reported that the range of intelligence is much broader in the older groups. This should not be a factor because those who enroll in your class are probably those with the higher test scores.

Perhaps Cattell (1963) provided a helpful suggestion when he compared "fluid" and "crystallized" intelligence. Fluid intelligence is reported as independent of education and experience. It involves the ability to recognize complex material and allows us to maintain entries in short-term memory which provides for more abstract reasoning. On the other hand, crystallized intelligence appears to develop from our combining fluid intelligence with experience. A broad vocabulary, a repertoire of coping techniques, and general information all compile our crystallized intelligence. While fluid intelligence peaks in our 20s, crystallized intelligence continues to increase into our 40s. Material presented at a slower pace that does not place too great a demand on short-term memory will enable older individuals to function comparably to younger classmates.

Another way to look at mental functioning is to differentiate between what Guilford (1956) terms divergent and convergent thinking. Divergent thinking occurs when students allow their thoughts to divert into different directions. This process results in a variety of original ideas and solutions to problems. Convergent thinking focuses on the best answer and tends to produce the most conventional response. Older adults are inclined to use the latter, convergent thinking. The typical objective test item requires convergent thought in that it normally has one conventional answer. It may be that one's form of thinking is very individualistic and sable over time; however, Hudson (1966) found divergent thinkers preferred studying liberal arts while convergent thinkers preferred studying science. Students generally benefit from exam questions that require them to utilize both of these thought processes.

The Instructor or Professor

In any classroom, the personality, characteristics, and history of the instructor set the tone for the class. Dealing with older students presents unique opportunities and responsibilities for instructors. If you were a returning student once upon a time, let it be known. This is a great reassurance and motivator for your older students. Personal reflections, unless they sound arrogant, are usually enjoyed by all students and can contribute to a relaxed classroom environment. You will often find that establishing classroom rapport with older students is easier. Because they have vast experiences and broad interests, it's easier to find a mutual bond on which to develop rapport.

Teaching students older than you can present a special challenge. Your being alert, enthusiastic, and eager to learn can motivate your students. Use your age and energy to enhance the educational experience for both your class and you.

Not only should you be interested in the subject but you should share your interest and enthusiasm. Follow up on class questions by providing resources or copies of material from your office. If you don't know the answer to a question, readily admit it -- but state that you are willing to study the issue. Encourage your students to independently research the information they question.

Be sure to allow time for students to approach you outside of class. Being available an hour or so before or after class is usually convenient for most students. Set regular hours for meeting with students and make sure you are available as scheduled. Don't get locked into your schedule so tightly that you become inflexible when students have legitimate conflicts with your schedule but still need time with you. Be responsive to the time demands of adults with multiple roles.

If you have taught for a while, you have probably encountered a few students with whom you have had real difficulty in communicating. It's not rational to expect to please all students nor for all students to respond to your teaching style. If you have tried and honestly feel you are not meeting the needs of a particular student, you may want to direct that student to another instructor for assistance. You and other instructors can work out the details among you.

Most college instructors have taken a limited number of speaking or teaching courses. It is important that we practice our delivery method. Attend workshops and seminars if possible. Limiting distracting mannerisms, practicing correct tone, and encouraging students to relax and learn are specific goals of the instruction process.

The Material, its Format and Presentation

Does the instructor need special abilities to successfully organize and present material for a diverse student population? No, special abilities are not necessary, but there are techniques that will further the educational experience for all students, especially the older ones. Much research has been done on this topic by psychologists and gerontologists. Results indicate that instructors should vary styles of teaching according to the needs of their students.

If some adult students appear slow, it may be because maturity tends to increase the use of reflective answers rather than the quicker, impulsive responses offered by younger students. The adults' efforts to reflect, evaluate, and select responses should not be interpreted as a lack of intelligence or ability. The following suggestions for teaching older students are based on research of educators such as Holmes (1982), Andrews (1981), and Meierhenry (1983):

--   Material should be organized for a logical flow.

--   Unnecessary clauses are frequently misunderstood.

--   Process approaches achieve greater adult cognitive learning than task approaches.

--   Use positive statements rather than negative.

--   Adults prefer participatory learning experiences.

--   Learners should be taken from the unknown to the known in short, clear steps.

--   Use action verbs.

--   Use short sentences; avoid long, wordy sentences.

--   Use vocabulary familiar to students.

-- Efficient and effective use of time is important to adults.
-- Always remain flexible and open.

-- Adults do better with self-directed learning.

-- Adults, more so than younger students, need to understand the purpose of learning specific material.

-- Remember time is a major variable in learning efficiently.

-- Encourage students to serve as resources for one another.

-- Provide alternative ways for accomplishing tasks.

-- Older students don't process visual information as rapidly as younger students. Allow more time when using slides and overhead displays.

-- Adult learners appear to be active learners. Materials should be first-hand and experience-based.

-- Instructors should use a variety of materials and offer many opportunities for both reflecting and doing.

-- The type of course and its subject require the instructor to make a special effort to increase or decrease structure. Obviously, science courses demand a certain level of structure. They may require considerable effort to minimize the structure and to be more open. On the other hand, the humanities are overly open with little structure and require attention to achieve an adequate balance of structure.

--   The materials selected depend on the subject matter, course objectives, and the recipients involved. Materials should be selected to provide interaction between you and the students, as well as among students.

--   Trigger or initiate discussions and encourage participation.

--   Harmonize differences, coordinate, and summarize views being presented.

--   Injecting personal comments or nonessential material in the lesson may liven the lecture or encourage students to relax; however, if done excessively, this may confuse older students. Be sure you separate such comments from the task at hand.

--   Processing information is slower for adult students; therefore, ideas should not be jumbled haphazardly but presented orderly and one at a time.

--   Maintain a moderate pace of speaking during lectures and replay important segments of taped materials.

--   Older students are traditionally cautious: they are more inclined to provide no response than to make a mistake. Reward their responses even if the particular comment was incorrect.

--   Exams are more stressful for older students. Extra effort should be made to assure that they understand the instructions.   On their jobs, accuracy has been stressed and older students tend to bring this emphasis to exams. For them, accuracy is more important than speed. With this in mind, you may want to reconsider the time requirements for exams.

Summary

Teaching older students is both rewarding and challenging. They bring their own expertise and maturity to the classroom. They also bring their own expectations, needs, and goals which are different from younger students'.   They ask for no special treatment but they expect to be "taught" on their level. With a little effort on the instructor's part, older students can relate "real world" reality to the theories and principles being discussed. Returning students are a welcome classroom resource that motivates both younger students and instructors.

References

Andrews, T. E. (1981). Improving Adult learning Programs. In Andrews, T. E., Houston, W. R., and Bryant, B. L. (eds.) Adult Learner. Washington, D. C.: Association of Teacher Educators.

Birren, J. E. (1964). The Psychology of Aging. Englewood Cliffs, NJ: Prentice-Hall.

Botwinick, J. (1978). Aging and Behavior (2nd ed.). New York: Springer.

Cattell, R. B. (1963). Theory of Fluid and Crystallized Intelligence: A Critical Experiment. Journal of Educational Psychology, 54, pp. 1-22.

Domjan, M., and Burkhard, B. (1986). The Principles of Learning and Behavior (2nd ed.). Monterey, CA: Brooks/Cole.

Erikson, E. H. (1950). Childhood and Society. New York: W. W. Norton.

Gould, R. (1978). Transformations. New York: Simon and Schuster.

Guilford, J. P. (1956). The Structure of Intellect. Psychological Bulletin, 43, pp. 267-293.

Holmes, N. (1982). The Readability of Study Materials: Recent Research in New Zealand. In J. S. Daniel, M. A. Stand, and J. R. Thompson (eds.) Learning at a Distance, A World Perspective. Edmonton, Alberta: Athabasca University-ICDE.

Hudson, L. (1966). Contrary Imaginations: A Psychological Study of the English Schoolboy. London: Methuen.

Hughes, J. A. and Graham, S. W. (1990). Adult Life Roles: A New Approach to Adult Development. The Journal of Continuing Higher Education, 38, no. 2, pp. 1-8.

Hughes, J. A., Graham, S. W., and Galbraith, M. W. (1986). Adult Development: A Multifacted Approach. The Journal of Continuing Higher Education, 34, no. 3, pp. 24-28.

Knowles, M. (1973). The Adult Learner: A Neglected Species (2nd ed.). Houston: Gulf.

McWhinney, W. (1990). Education for the Third Quarter of Life. The Journal of Continuing Higher Education, 38, no. 2, pp. 14-20.

Meierhenry, W. C. (1983). Educational Materials for Teaching Adults. In J. P. Wilson (ed.) Materials for Teaching Adults: Selection, Development, and Use. San Francisco: Jossey-Bass.

Roberts, D. M. (1968). Abilities and Learning: A Brief Review and Discussion of Empirical Studies. Journal of School Psychology, 7, pp. 12-21.

Sheehy, G. (1974). Passages: Predictable Crisis of Adult Life. New York: Dutton.

APPENDIX A

SUGGESTED READINGS

Allen, Charlotte. Daddy's Girl. New York: Berkley, 1980.

Andrews, T. E., Houston, W. R., and Bryant, B. L. Adult Learners. Washington D C: Association of Teachers Education, 1981.

Amada, Gerald. A Guide to Psychotherapy New York: Madison Books, 1985.

Apps, Jerold W. The Adult Learner on Campus: A Guide for Instructors and Administrators. Chicago: Follett, 1981.

Bass, Ellen. I Never Told Anyone: A Collection of Writings by Women Survivors of Child Sexual Abuse. New York: Harper and Row, 1983.

Bass, Ellen and Davis, Laura. The Courage to Heal. New York: Harper and Row, 1988.

Beattie, Melody. Co-Dependent No More. Center City, Minn.: Hazeldon, 1987.

Bernard, J. The Future of Marriage. New York: Bantam, 1972.

Black, Claudia. It Will Never Happen to Me: Children of Alcoholics. Denver: MAC Publishing, 1981.

Blume, E. S. Secret Survivors, New York: John Wiley and Sons, 1990.

Borcherdt, Bill. Think Straight! Feel Great!. Sarasota, FL: Professional Resource Exchange, 1989.

Bradshaw, John. Bradshaw on: Healing the Shame That Binds You. Deerfield Beach, FL.: Health Communications, 1988.

Bradshaw, John. Homecoming: Reclaiming Championing Your Inner Child. New York: Bantam, 1990.

Brady, Katherine. Father's Days. New York: Dell, 1981.

Briggs, Dorothy C.   Your Child's Self-Esteem: Step-by-Step Guidelines to Raising Responsible, Productive, Happy Children. Garden City, N. Y.: Doubleday, 1970.

Brownmiller, Susan. Against Our Will. New York: Bantam, 1976.

Butler, Sandra. Conspiracy of Silence: The Trauma of Incest. San Francisco: Volcano Press, 1985.

Caplan, Paula J. The Myth of Women's Masochism. New York: E. P. Dutton, 1985.

Cermak, Timmen.   A Primer on Adult Children of Alcoholics. Pompano Beach, FL.: Health Communications, 1985.

Cheinin, Kim.   The Obsession: Reflections on the Tyranny of Slenderness. New York: Harper and Row, 1981.

Cheinin, Kim. The Hungry Self: Women, Eating and Identity, New York: Times Books, 1985.

Colgrove, Melba, Bloomfield, Harold, and McWilliams, Peter. How to Survive the Loss of a Love. New York: Bantam, 1976.

Courtois, Christine A. Healing the Incest Wound: Adult Survivors in Therapy. New York: W. W. Norton & Co., 1988.

Crewdson, John. By Silence Betrayed: Sexual Abuse of Children in America. Boston: Little, Brown and Company, 1988.

Crosson-Tower, Cynthia. Secret Scars: A Guide for Survivors of Child Sexual Abuse. New York: Viking, 1988.

Daugherty, Lynn. Why Me? Racine, Wis.: Mother Courage Press, 1984.

Ellis, Albert and Dryden, Windy. The Practice of Rational Emotive Therapy. New York: Springer, 1987.

Ellis, Albert and Harper, Robert. A New Guide to Rational Living. Hollywood: Wilshire, 1961.

Faelton, Sharon and Diamond, David. Tenson Turnaround. Emmaus, PA: Rodale, 1990.

Finkelhor, David. Child Sexual Abuse. New York: The Free Press, 1984.

Fisher, Bruce. Rebuilding. San Luis Olispo, CA: Impact, 1981.

Fortune, Marie M. Sexual Violence: The unmentionable Sin: An Ethical and Pastoral Perspective. New York: Pilgrim, 1983.

Forward, Susan and Buck, Craig. Betrayal of Innocence: Incest and Its Devastation. New York: Penguin, 1979.

Fraser, Sylvia. My Father's House: A Memoir of Incest and of Healing. New York: Ticknor and Fields, 1988.

Gendlin, Eugene. Focusing. New York: Bantam, 1981.

Gil, Eliana. Outgrowing the Pain. San Francisco: Launch, 1984.

Goodwin, Jean M. Sexual Abuse: Incest Victims and Their Families. Littleton, Mass.: Wright-PSG, 1982.

Hancock, Maxine, and Mains, Karen. Child Sexual Abuse: A Hope for Healing. Wheaton, Ill.: Harold Shaw, 1987.

Haponski, W. C. and McCabe, C. E. Back to School: The College Guide for Adults. Princeton: Peterson's Guides, 1985.

Hay, Louise. You Can Heal Your Life. Santa Monica: Hay House, 1984.

Herman, Judith L. Father-Daughter Incest. Cambridge: Harvard Press, 1982.

Kaufman, Gershen. Shame: The Power of Caring. Cambridge: Schenkman Books, 1980.

Kempe, Ruth S. and Kempe, C. H. Child Abuse. Cambridge: Harvard Press, 1978.

Knowles, Malcolm. The Adult learner: A Neglected Species, (2nd ed), Houston: Gulf, 1978.

Knox, Alan B. (Ed). Jossey-Bass Higher Education Series. San Francisco: Jossey-Bass, 1982.

Komarovsky, Mirra. Women In College: Shaping New Feminine Identities. New York: Basic, 1985.

Lerner, Harriet G. The Dance of Anger: A Women's Guide to Changing the Patterns of Intimate Relationships. New York: Harper and Row, 1986.

Lovell, R. B. Adult Learning, New York: John Wiley and Sons, 1980.

Lyng, R. D. and Gerow, J. R. How to Succeed in College. 2nd ed. London: Scott, Foresman and Company, 1986.

Martin, Del Battered Wives. San Francisco: Glide, 1976.

McKay, Mathew, et al. The Relaxation and Stress Reduction Workbook. Oakland: New Harbinger, 1988.

Meiselman, Karin. Incest: A Psychological Study of Causes and Effects with Treatment Recommendations. San Francisco: Jossey-Bass, 1978.

Merriam, Sharon B. and Simpson, Edwin L. A Guide to Research for Educators and Trainers of Adults. Malabar, FL.: Robert Krieger, 1989.

Michelson, Larry and Ascher, L. M. (Eds) Anxiety and Stress Disorders. New York: Guilford Press, 1987.

Miller, Alice. <u>For Your Own Good</u>. New York: Farrar, Straus, and Girou, 1983.

Newcomer, Mabel. <u>A Century of Higher Education for Women</u>. New York: Harper and Row, 1959.

Morris, Michele. <u>If I Should Die Before I Wake</u>. New York: Dell, 1982.

Norwood, Robin. <u>Women Who Love Too Much</u>. Los Angeles: Jeremy Tarcher, 1985.

Peck, M. S. <u>The Road Less Traveled</u>. New York: Simon and Schuster, 1978.

Phelps, S. and Austin, N. <u>The Assertive Woman: A New Look</u>. San Luis Obispo: Impact, 1987.

Pilkonis, Paul. The behavioral consequence of shyness. <u>Journal of Personality</u>, <u>45</u>, 596-611, 1979.

Poloma, M. M. Role conflict and the married professional woman. In C. Safilios-Rothschild (ed.), <u>Toward a Sociology of Women</u>. Lexington: Xerox, 1972.

Renvoize, Jean. <u>Incest: A Family Pattern</u>. London: Routledge and Kegan Paul, 1982.

Roth, Geneen. <u>Why Weight?</u> New York: Plume, 1989.

Roth, Geneen. <u>Feeding the Hungry Heart: The Experience of Compulsive Eating</u>. New York: Bobbs-Merrill, 1982.

Russell, Diana. <u>Sexual Exploitation: Rape, Child Sexual Abuse, Workplace Harassment</u>, Newbury Park, CA.: Sage, 1984.

Rush, Florence. <u>The Best-Kept Secret: Sexual Abuse of Children</u>. Englewood Cliffs, N.J.: Prentice-Hall, 1980.

Sanford, Linda. The Silent Children: A Parent's Guide to the
    Prevention of Child Sexual Abuse. New York: McGraw-Hill,
    1982.

Sanford, Linda and Donovan, Mary. Women and Self-Esteem:
    Understanding and Improving the Way We Think and Feel
    about Ourselves. New York: Penguin, 1986.

Schaef, Anne W. Co-Dependence: Misunderstood--Mistreated.
    New York: Harper and Row, 1986.

Schaef, Anne W. Women's Reality. San Francisco: Harper and
    Row, 1985.

Shainess, Natalie. Sweet Suffering. New York: Bobbs-Merrill,
    1984.

Spielberger, Charles D. (Ed.) Anxiety and Behavior. New York:
    Academic, 1966.

Tavris, C. and Wade, C. The Longest War. New York: Harcourt
    Brace Jovanovich, 1984.

Viorst, Judith. Necessary Losses: The Loves, Illusions,
    Dependencies, and Impossible Expectations That All of Us
    Have to Give Up in Order to Grow. New York: Simon and
    Schuster, 1986.

Walker, Lenora E. The Battered Woman. New York: Harper and
    Row, 1979.

Wegscheider-Cruse, Sharon. Choice-Making: For Co-Dependents,
    Adult Children, and Spirituality Seekers. Pompano Beach:
    Health Communications, 1985.

Wegscheider-Cruse, Sharon. Learning to Love Yourself: Finding
    Your Self-Worth.   Pompano Beach: Health
    Communications, 1987.

Whitfield, Charles. Healing the Child Within. Pompano Beach: Health Communications, 1987.

Wolpe, Joseph. The Practice of Behavior Therapy. 4th ed. New York: Pergamon, 1990.

Woodley, Alan, Wagner, Maria, Hamilton, Mary, and Fulton, Oliver. Choosing to Learn: Adults in Education. Philadelphia: SRHE and Open University Press, 1987.

APPENDIX B
SCHEDULE CHART

HOUR	MON	TUES	WED	THUR	FRI	SAT	SUN
7:00							
7:30							
8:00							
8:30							
9:00							
9:30							
10:00							
10:30							
11:00							
11:30							
12:00							
12:30							
1:00							
1:30							
2:00							
2:30							
3:00							
3:30							
4:00							
4:30							
5:00							
5:30							
6:00							
6:30							
7:00							
7:30							
8:00							
8:30							
9:00							
9:30							
10:00							

CONTRIBUTORS

*Guinevera Nance, Ph.D., University of Virginia
Vice Chancellor of Academic Affairs, Auburn University at Montgomery. Professor of English. Author of Aldous Huxley (1988) and co-author of Philip Roth (1991), concise biographical critical studies of the men and their works.

*Susan Dudley, Ph.D., University of Massachusetts
Assistant Professor of psychology, University of Maryland - Spain. Specialty areas include psychophysiology and women's issues.

*Linda Jenkins, M.S., Jacksonville State University
Director of Student Development, Auburn University at Montgomery. Founder of successful orientation programs and extended programs for returning students.

*Carolyn Long, M.S., University of Georgia
Assistant Professor of Psychology, Auburn University at Montgomery. Licensed Professional Counselor. Specialties include learning and addictions.

*Eugenie Nickell, M.S., Auburn University at Montgomery
Outpatient Therapist-Psychometrist. Alabama Mental Health Center, Vernon, AL. Co-author of "It's Never Too Late (1988), a guide for older non-traditional students.

*Carolyn Thomas, Ph.D., University of Iowa
Director of Counseling Center, Auburn University at Montgomery. Associate Professor of Education. Licensed Professional Counselor. Specialties include domestic abuse and women's issues.

*Del Witherspoon, M.S., Auburn University
Instructor of Psychology, Auburn University at Montgomery. Co-author of It's Never Too Late (1988), a guide for older non-traditional students.

*Earned degree as an older, non-traditional student.